Does Deconstruction Make Any Difference?

Does Deconstruction Make Any Difference?

Poststructuralism and the Defense of Poetry in Modern Criticism

MICHAEL FISCHER

INDIANA UNIVERSITY PRESS • BLOOMINGTON

Copyright © 1985 by Michael Fischer

Manufactured in the United States of America

Library of Congress Cataloging in Publication Data

Fischer, Michael, 1949–
Does deconstruction make any difference?

Bibliography: p.
Includes index.
1. Criticism.   2. Deconstruction.   I. Title.
PN81.F545   1985   801'.95   84-48044
ISBN 0-253-31810-6

1 2 3 4 5   89 88 87 86 85

For Kim

Contents

ACKNOWLEDGMENTS

It is a pleasure to thank the many people who have helped me with this book. Marta Field patiently typed (and retyped) the manuscript. Hugh Witemeyer, Sam Girgus, Hoyt Trowbridge, E. D. Hirsch, Jr., and Christopher Lasch read parts of the manuscript and offered valuable encouragement and advice. I am especially indebted to the friendship and guidance of Morris Eaves and Gerald Graff, who have read virtually everything I have written, including several versions of this book. Finally, I want to thank my children, Joshua and Sarah, not only for prolonging this project but also for enriching it.

INTRODUCTION

Does Deconstruction Make Any Difference? connects several concerns often kept apart: current arguments on behalf of the indeterminacy of literary texts; the attempts of Matthew Arnold and Northrop Frye to justify literary criticism; and recent developments in the academic study of literature, such as declining enrollments in literature courses and dwindling opportunities in teaching. Because some readers may suspect that in previous criticism these topics have been kept apart because they belong apart, I shall try to explain why I am bringing them together here.

I am chiefly concerned with the claim of many contemporary critics that "a text never has a single meaning, but is a crossroads of multiple ambiguous meanings. . . . It cannot be reduced to a single, univocal statement but is 'equivocal' or 'multivocal,' " to quote J. Hillis Miller. Deconstruction, of course, has influenced many of the critics who make such a claim but not all of them, as the example of Harold Bloom shows. In this book I am focusing not only on deconstruction but on the larger tendencies that deconstruction epitomizes— tendencies that in various ways call into question our capacity to decide on the meaning of literary (and nonliterary) texts. The movement from "deconstruction" to "poststructuralism" in my title thus indicates my interest in Bloom, Stanley Fish, Geoffrey Hartman, and other critics who, though not deconstructionists, endorse some of the skeptical assumptions about meaning that deconstruction takes to an extreme. Instead of focusing on the differences among these critics, I will be examining an assumption that they have in common—the assumption that works of literature are in some sense indeterminate.

In asking whether "deconstruction makes any difference," I assume that deconstructionists, by contesting the "decidability" of meaning, are trying to make a positive difference in the ways that we treat works of literature. It is true that instead of defending literature, deconstructionists usually say that they are attacking it, in particular its privileged status as special discourse, its traditional function as a repository of humanistic values, and its solidity as a cultural institution. But, from the point of view of deconstruction, this apparent demotion of literature actually liberates it from explanatory schemata that have stifled it. Though meant to protect literature, deconstructionists argue, the barriers put around literature have kept it tame, protecting us from its disruption of the "truths," however complex, imposed on it. Redefined as open-ended writing, literature, in deconstruction, is not a servile instrument but an unruly force that we wrongfully, but understandably, have sought to contain.

"We" here refers to academic critics, "moldy fig academics," as Harold Bloom has called them (or us). Disdain for the narrowness, drudgery, and pointlessness of academic criticism partly motivates deconstruction and accounts for its considerable appeal, especially among disaffected academics who see themselves as either outside the profession or above it: young Ph.D.'s denied teaching jobs, publication, or tenure by a seemingly arbitrary, self-serving consensus; women and minorities who wish to expand an apparently inert, irrelevant curriculum; expository writing specialists and interdisciplinary scholars who want to put the similarities between literature and other kinds of writing at the center, not at the periphery or in the basement, of literary study; and established critics who hope to free interpretation from the mechanical reduction of texts to bland statements that uninformed, unmotivated students can digest.

While indebted to other studies of deconstruction, mine places it in the context of the grievances that I have been citing. In my view, many readers have unfairly maligned deconstruction as an airy theoretical nothing, indifferent to the many practical difficulties that plague the academic profession, among them "the uncomfortably hermetic quality" of contemporary literary scholarship, the lopsided concern for publication rather than teaching, "the growing vocationalism of the young," the waning of literacy, and the misplaced priorities of American society, which withholds funds from colleges "on the verge of bankruptcy," while seldom begrudging money "for the subsidization of plants manufacturing bombers, nuclear submarines, or napalm" (I quote from a series of books on the profession published by the Association of Departments of English). Deconstruction, as I try to show, not only is aware of these problems but responds to them by contesting the boundaries that currently imprison texts. It thus validates the

widespread feeling that literary study has been hemmed in by claustrophobic fictions born of accident and error.

I criticize deconstructionists in chapter 5 not for objecting to the
academic status quo but for undermining their own objections by
questioning the cognitive status of literature and criticism. The
weapon that, in deconstruction, frees literature—the "undecidability"
of meaning—ends up further accommodating literature to the
academic establishment that deconstructionists resent. Put differently,
deconstruction, as I view it, mirrors the conditions that it rightly
criticizes: hence its complicity with the interpretive community that at
first glance it seems to repudiate. Deconstruction, I argue in chapter
6, does make a difference, though not the difference that many of its
enemies and advocates have thus far supposed. Instead of endanger-
ing the academic profession, deconstruction leaves it intact, maybe
even more secure.

In addition to discussing some of the institutional ramifications of
deconstruction, I am also interested here in its intellectual origins.
Instead of searching for these origins in such obvious precursors of
deconstruction as Nietzsche, Saussure, Freud, and Heidegger—all of
them the subject of much recent work—I turn in my first two chapters
to two critics who try to resist many of the developments that deconstruction accelerates: Matthew Arnold and Northrop Frye. Friends of
deconstruction typically vilify Arnold and Frye as enemies, while foes
of deconstruction often call on them as antidotes to the nihilism that
presumably threatens us. But both factions agree that deconstruction,
for better or for worse, represents a decisive break with the human-
ism of Arnold and the optimism of Frye. While not denying the
novelty of deconstruction, I try to show that the forces that have
erupted in deconstruction have already been there, if not everywhere
in the history of criticism, then at least in some of the major critical
theorists of the nineteenth and twentieth centuries, even Arnold and
Frye. In these first two chapters I am not abandoning the more immediate concerns of the rest of my book, but stepping back from
them, seeing deconstruction along with the current crisis in literary
study as the latest episodes in a story that has been going on at least
since the nineteenth century.

I conclude on an admittedly negative note, charging several poststructuralist critics with perpetuating what they rightly deplore. Even
so, I would not characterize my argument as pessimistic: my point is

not simply that deconstruction is costly, but that it is also unwarranted. As I argue in chapters 3 and 4, there is nothing epistemologically necessary or historically inevitable about the tendencies in deconstruction that I find so damaging. Although the study of literature is difficult to defend—as the examples of Arnold and Frye illustrate—it is not impossible. In attacking the skepticism of Derrida and others, I am, then, taking a preliminary step toward reconstituting the claim that these writers have weakened, especially Frye's claim that "the ethical purpose of a liberal education is to liberate, which can only mean to make one capable of conceiving society as free, classless, and urbane."

In calling my book a preliminary step, I mean, first, that I am less interested here in mounting a full-scale defense of literature than in showing what such a defense must entail, namely, respect for the determinacy and referentiality of literary texts. Put very simply, I try to show that instead of liberating or shoring up literature, questioning our capacity to determine and trust what a text says weakens its authority. Second, my book is preliminary in the sense that much of its energy goes into exposing the weaknesses of the critical positions that it attacks. I am well aware that much more work needs to be done to show that the realist aesthetic that I favor can be successfully argued for—that it is more coherent and persuasive than the non- or antirealist theories that I criticize.

The realist or mimetic theory that I am advocating here will not reject deconstruction but work through it, conserving its strengths, in particular its justifiable dissatisfaction with much that we regard as necessary or natural in contemporary academic criticism (for example, the sequestering of literature from "extrinsic" texts and concerns) and its conviction that literary works do not lend themselves to absolutely certain interpretations that sum them up once and for all. The kind of argument toward which my book leads is perhaps best suggested by the work of Stanley Cavell, who adumbrates a way of appropriating the insights of skepticism while transcending its limitations. In *Does Deconstruction Make Any Difference?*, however, I am mainly interested in the legitimacy and the cost of undermining the cognitive value of literature and criticism; elsewhere I hope to show how a philosopher like Cavell points a way out of the dead end to which deconstruction leads.

Does Deconstruction Make Any Difference?

I

Matthew Arnold and Contemporary Criticism

In *Anatomy of Criticism,* Northrop Frye pictures literary criticism as "an imaginary stock exchange" in which the "reputations of poets boom and crash."[1] If criticism resembles Wall Street, then the stock of Matthew Arnold is at an all-time low, at least among poststructuralists. In *Criticism in the Wilderness,* Geoffrey Hartman's spirited defense of "revisionist" criticism, Arnold stands for nearly everything that many current critics (Hartman among them) repudiate, especially the separation of criticism from literature, the imposition on criticism of stultifying pedagogical and social ends, and the consequent suppression of the critic's creativity, daring, enthusiasm, and playfulness, an impoverishment of criticism that Hartman derisively calls the "Arnoldian concordat." "By its very existence, as well as its peculiar features," the criticism of today, in Hartman's words, is breaking down "this defensive partition of the critical and the creative spirit, which recognizes the intelligence of the creative writer but refuses the obverse proposition that there may be creative force in the critical writer. . . ."[2]

Hartman, I should add, does compliment Arnold for displaying "range and freedom" despite his stifling theories (*CW,* 175). Arnold emphasized objective, unadorned critical writing, moreover, in part because he understandably recoiled from the irresponsibility of some of his predecessors:

> If I say, echoing Spenser, that critics should have the kingdom of their language, it does not follow that one should always write in a heightened style or return to the brutality of the journals and the vulgarity of the newspapers of which Arnold complained. To read early nine-

1

teenth-century reviews of the romantics might turn one into an Arnoldian sophisticate on the spot. (*CW,* 157)

And Arnold responded enthusiastically to Continental writers, anticipating the cosmopolitanism of Paul de Man and others. Still, despite
these points in Arnold's favor, Hartman's presentation of him is negative—so much so that a quick reference to a critic's affinities with
Arnold becomes a shorthand way of registering that critic's limitations
(as when Hartman notes that "Northrop Frye in *Fearful Symmetry*
[1947] corrected rather than challenged the post-Arnoldian point of
view" [*CW,* 87]). Hartman accordingly takes the title of his book from a
famous statement in "The Function of Criticism at the Present Time":

> The epochs of Aeschylus and Shakespeare make us feel their pre-
> eminence. In an epoch like those is, no doubt, the true life of litera-
> ture; there is the promised land, toward which criticism can only
> beckon. That promised land it will not be ours to enter, and we shall die
> in the wilderness: but to have saluted it from afar, is already, perhaps,
> the best distinction among contemporaries; it will certainly be the best
> title to esteem with posterity.

For Hartman, "this wilderness is all we have" (*CW,* 15). Criticism today—speculative, playful, and wide-ranging—*is* that literature for
which Arnold thought critics could only prepare.

Arnold, to be sure, has his defenders, many of whom use his work
to attack the very developments that Hartman champions. In "Arnold
at the Present Time," Eugene Goodheart's contribution to a recent
Critical Inquiry symposium on Arnold's work, Arnold becomes a
touchstone against which we can measure "the devaluation of literary
experience in modern critical theory (particularly in its deconstructionist version)." In Goodheart's opinion, "it is fair to say that advanced literary critics in their corrosive skepticism about meaning and
language have in effect abdicated their responsibility to what might be
called the social question of the humanities. Arnold remains an em-
blem of that responsibility."[3] In "Arnold Then and Now: The Use and
Misuse of Criticism," Morris Dickstein similarly finds in Arnold an
alternative to "the decline of criticism" begun in the 1950s and ac-
celerated by "today's new formalists," who

> seem to exalt criticism yet actually undermine it by attacking its truth-
> telling function—by vaporizing the literary object while endlessly mul-
> tiplying opportunities for redescribing it. Criticism has promoted itself

by sacrificing an essential part of its *raison d'être;* never has it received so much attention at the *expense* of literature. Arnold, anticipating Derrida, described the object of criticism as "of all things the most volatile, elusive, and evanescent." But he never fell into skepticism or nihilism, despite the darker forces, modern anxieties, and elegiac moods at work in his poetry.

Impressed, like Goodheart, by the air of authority that pervades Arnold's work, Dickstein concludes that literary study today, by contrast, "has lost its old connection with conduct" and therefore lacks any clear rationale.[4]

In subsequent chapters I will be criticizing deconstruction along similar lines. Here, however, I want to contest the image of Arnold upheld by both Hartman's censure and Goodheart's and Dickstein's praise. Whereas Hartman opts for play, Goodheart and Dickstein obviously prefer straightforward seriousness, finding speculative skepticism self-indulgent and debilitating rather than fun. But all three critics impute to Arnold a sobriety and sense of duty that stem from his allegedly firm conviction that his criticism matters. Arnold, in this view, is serious because he has to be (or because he can be): he knows that his judgments bear not just on literary questions but on the practical decisions that his readers face. In my view, these critics credit Arnold with a single-mindedness, effectiveness, and self-confidence that he may have coveted but seldom displayed. While they concede that Arnold equivocated even in his most optimistic pronouncements, they do not see that his doubts threatened and in some ways undermined his defense of literature.

At stake in this discussion of Arnold is, first, a historical point: Arnold's work represents neither a golden age from which criticism has declined nor a repressive past from which it has cleanly broken.[5] The ambivalence and doubts that inform contemporary criticism are already there in Arnold, disrupting the intentions that recent critics think that he carried out. I am also trying here to make the theoretical point that any defense of literature—more exactly, any defense of the importance of literature to action—has to reinforce the cognitive pretensions of literature that atrophy in Arnold's work. By hedging on the truth claims of literature, Arnold weakened the connection between literature and conduct that he tried to secure.

The best approach to Arnold's thought is through Frederic Harrison, or, more precisely, through the contempt for culture that Harrison expressed in an 1867 *Fortnightly Review* article quoted in *Culture and Anarchy*. Culture, Harrison charged,

> is a desirable quality in a critic of new books, and sits well on a professor of *belles-lettres;* but as applied to politics, it means simply a turn for small fault-finding, love of selfish ease, and indecision in action. The man of culture is in politics one of the poorest mortals alive. For simple pedantry and want of good sense no man is his equal. No assumption is too unreal, no end is too unpractical for him. But the active exercise of politics requires common sense, sympathy, trust, resolution, and enthusiasm, qualities which your man of culture has carefully rooted up, lest they damage the delicacy of his critical olfactories. Perhaps they are the only class of responsible beings in the community who cannot with safety be entrusted with power.[6]

Harrison's association of culture with nit-picking, indolence, and snobbishness reflected (at least in Arnold's eyes) the unpoetic spirit of the age, especially its positivism and utilitarianism. Literature seemed "unreal" because unscientific, "unpractical" because unprofitable. It could claim no credit for the expansion of commerce, production, technology, and population, all the developments that "the modern spirit" prized.

Arnold, of course, opposed the denigration of culture that Harrison celebrated. He saw that the alleged impracticality of culture, for example, originated in the degradation of work. Because making a living depended on mindless submission to a fixed routine, the arts, which value other qualities, seemed a waste of time. For Arnold, the "exclusive worship" of industry was ineluctably destructive because "narrow and mechanical" (*CA,* 186–87). Competing for employment, working at specialized tasks, and sticking to a preestablished plan cost workers their creativity, spontaneity, and wholeness even when it brought their employers profits. More money and more leisure could assuage these losses but never could make up for them.

When Arnold made these criticisms in 1867, they were neither new nor trite. In *The Stones of Venice* (1851–53), John Ruskin had protested against the division of labor ("It is not, truly speaking, the labour that is divided; but the men"); the subordination of men to machines ("You must either make a tool of the creature, or a man of him. You cannot make both"); and the separation of invention from execution, intellectual from manual labor:

> We are always in these days endeavouring to separate the two; we want one man to be always thinking, and another to be always working, and we call one a gentleman, and the other an operative; whereas the workman ought often to be thinking, and the thinker often to be working, and both should be gentlemen, in the best sense. As it is, we make both ungentle, the one envying, the other despising, his brother; and the mass of society is made up of morbid thinkers, and miserable workers. Now it is only by labour that thought can be made healthy, and only by thought that labour can be made happy, and the two cannot be separated with impunity.[7]

As early as 1844 Karl Marx had deplored the alienation of labor and, still earlier, the English romantics and William Cobbett, Robert Owen, and other reformers had lamented the squalor, competitiveness, and inequalities of modern society. Arnold departed from these other critics of society, especially from the romantics, not so much in his diagnosis as in his solutions: literary criticism and education.

Put very simply, critics and teachers, in Arnold's view, transmit the moral values (wholeness, harmony, and growth, for example) that great literary and philosophical texts endorse. Arnold conceded to "believers in action" like Harrison that critics and educators have to detach themselves from the practical concerns of their day. But this retreat from immediate matters allows concentration on larger ones; it gives critics the chance to formulate authentic norms and to make them prevail. Though ends in themselves, reading, observing, thinking, teaching, and writing also remake the world by providing the "basis for a less confused action and a more complete perfection than we have at present" (*CA*, 191).

As a critic, Arnold was not so much abandoning poetry as creating that moment when good poetry could again be written. By "good" poetry he meant morally effective, "animating" poetry that leads to constructive action, not (like his own poem "Empedocles on Etna") to frustration or despair. As Arnold wrote to his friend Arthur Hugh Clough,

> I am glad you like the Gipsy Scholar—but what does it *do* for you? Homer *animates*—Shakespeare *animates*—in its poor way I think Sohrab and Rustum *animates*—the Gipsy Scholar at best awakens a pleasing melancholy. But this is not what we want.
>
>> The complaining millions of men
>> Darken in labour and pain—
>
> what they want is something to *animate* and *ennoble* them—not merely

to add zest to their melancholy or grace to their dreams.—I believe a
feeling of this kind is the basis of my nature—and of my poetics.[8]

Because poetry communicates rather than discovers ideas, however,
its effectiveness depends in part on an intellectual atmosphere already at the poet's disposal:

> The grand work of literary genius is a work of synthesis and exposi-
> tion, not of analysis and discovery; its gift lies in the faculty of being
> happily inspired by a certain intellectual and spiritual atmosphere, by a
> certain order of ideas, when it finds itself in them. . . . This is why great
> creative epochs in literature are so rare, this is why there is so much
> that is unsatisfactory in the productions of many men of real genius;
> because, for the creation of a masterwork of literature two powers
> must concur, the power of the man and the power of the moment, and
> the man is not enough without the moment; the creative power has, for
> its happy exercise, appointed elements, and those elements are not in
> its own control. ("The Function of Criticism at the Present Time," III,
> 261)

These elements "are more within the control of the critical power":
"Thus it tends, at last, to make an intellectual situation of which the
creative power can profitably avail itself. It tends to establish an order
of ideas," which, when they reach society, stimulate "a stir and growth
everywhere." "Out of this stir and growth come the creative epochs of
literature" ("The Function of Criticism at the Present Time," III,
261).

Because the romantics lacked a suitable "intellectual situation" (Arnold's argument concludes), their work was "premature," a victim of
the milieu that it tried to change. The fragmentation that the romantics deplored in their society reappeared in their literary remedies:
"This makes Byron so empty of matter, Shelley so incoherent,
Wordsworth even, profound as he is, yet so wanting in completeness
and variety" ("The Function of Criticism," III, 262). Although Arnold
is obviously criticizing the romantics, he is quarreling over means, not
ends. Criticism will accomplish what romantic poetry failed to bring
about: the "humanization" of a class-divided, "mechanical" society.

I have been describing what Hartman calls the Arnoldian concordat, the division of labor between criticism and poetry that Arnold set
up in "The Function of Criticism at the Present Time." I agree with
Hartman that this arrangement diminishes criticism, not, however, by
hobbling the critic's "creativity" (as Hartman would have it), but by

weakening the "truth-telling function" that, in Dickstein's view, criticism in Arnold serves. By making the discovery of new ideas the exclusive "business of the philosopher," Arnold threatened the ability of poetry to fulfill the social functions that he wanted it to assume.

At times, it appears as if Arnold expected poets to take dictation rather than to think. When poets usurp the role of philosophers, their work suffers. Wordsworth's philosophizing only results in "a tissue of elevated but abstract verbiage, alien to the very nature of poetry": "we cannot do him justice until we dismiss his formal philosophy" (IX, 48–49). Clough's efforts to "*solve* the Universe" similarly cast doubt on his "being an artist."[9] In rebuking Wordsworth and Clough, Arnold put poetry in its place, diffusing knowledge rather than adding to it.

Despite Arnold's references to the "high seriousness" of poetry, it is not even clear that truth describes what the poet teaches. In "Maurice de Guérin," Arnold observed that

> The grand power of poetry is its interpretive power; by which I mean, not a power of drawing out in black and white an explanation of the mystery of the universe, but the power of so dealing with things as to awaken in us a wonderfully full, new, and intimate sense of them, and of our relations with them. When this sense is awakened in us, as to objects without us, we feel ourselves to be in contact with the essential nature of those objects, to be no longer bewildered and oppressed by them, but to have their secret, and to be in harmony with them; and this feeling calms and satisfies us as no other can. . . . I will not now inquire whether this sense is illusive, whether it can be proved not to be illusive, whether it does absolutely make us possess the real nature of things; all I say is, that poetry can awaken it in us, and that to awaken it is one of the highest powers of poetry. (III, 12–13)

Arnold did not inquire into the sense of reality that we get from poetry because he felt that he did not have to; the power of poetry supposedly does not depend on our accepting it as true to "the real nature of things." We are calmed, satisfied, and fortified despite what we may believe about the poem's representation of the "objects around us."[10]

When Arnold discussed the evaluation of poetry, he similarly stopped short. For poetry to fulfill its social function, the best works must receive our attention: "The best poetry is what we want; the best poetry will be found to have a power of forming, sustaining, and delighting us, as nothing else can" ("The Study of Poetry," IX, 163).

Comparing a poem with lines of great poetry allows the critic to make a "real," as opposed to a "historical" or "personal," estimate of its value. Arnold realized that such a procedure begs the question of choosing the "infallible" touchstones, the "lines and expressions of the great masters" that serve as guides. But he refused to spell out his criteria:

> Critics give themselves great labor to draw out what in the abstract constitutes the characters of a high quality of poetry. It is much better simply to have recourse to concrete examples; to take specimens of poetry of the high, the very highest quality, and to say: The characters of a high quality of poetry are what is expressed *there.* They are far better recognized by being felt in the verse of the master, than by being perused in the prose of the critic. ("The Study of Poetry," IX, 170–71)

By going on to suggest that the greatness of a poem lies in its "manner" and "substance" (where else?), he hinted that he could define greatness if he desired (or if "urgently pressed"). But he did not want to: instead of further inquiring into the excellence of his touchstones, he praised their "high beauty, worth, and power," relocating the problem instead of solving it.

In Arnold, then, value judgments, like poems, are better felt than probed. At best, analysis is dispensable (we do not need to know whether the sense of reality we get from a poem is true); at worst, analysis clouds the questions it seeks to resolve (concrete examples define literary excellence better than abstract prose). I think that Arnold tried to bypass analysis in these instances because he feared it. Having already (in his view) corroded the authority of Christian dogma, rational inquiry could also jeopardize the social claims he wanted to make for the study of literature. Apologists for Christianity had unabashedly "materialized" its values in such "facts" as God, the creation, and the Resurrection. Now these facts were cracking under the pressure of Darwinian science and historical criticism:

> There is not a creed which is not shaken, not an accredited dogma which is not shown to be questionable, not a received tradition which does not threaten to dissolve. Our religion has materialized itself in the fact, in the supposed fact; it has attached its emotion to the fact, and now the fact is failing it. But for poetry the idea is everything; the rest is a world of illusion, of divine illusion. Poetry attaches its emotion to the idea; the idea *is* the fact. ("The Study of Poetry," IX, 161)

To avoid the fate of religious dogma, defenders of literature would make no statements about the external world that science could challenge: for literary critics, the "idea" would be everything. ("Idea" is significantly vague here. I am not sure what remains in a poem when we subtract its "facts," although presumably for Arnold its emotional and moral effect survives.) More precisely, literary works do not have to make statements that the scientist or historian can dispute because the effect of a work does not depend on its accurate representation of reality. By jettisoning cognitive claims for literature—claims that would only get literature in trouble—critics could preserve its social usefulness.

Or so Arnold hoped: his evasive approach to the truth of literature, in fact, weakened what he tried to save. As Lionel Trilling argued in *Matthew Arnold* (1938),

> Men will not, after all, rest in the validity of their emotions merely; perhaps it is only the observer and philosopher who can regard these, with a hint of patronage, as sufficient. . . . [H]owever much the poetic experience may order our lives, however much pseudo-statement may organize our emotions, its effect is not so great as that of "statement" or what we firmly believe to be statement.[11]

Trilling suggests—and I agree—that a poem has to earn its right to influence us by respecting or adding to our knowledge. I take this point to be an empirical one, founded on an observation that mimetic critics often make, namely, that people take truth more seriously than fiction, though they of course differ in what they regard as fantastic and real. "Seriously" here measures the effect of discourse on actions: we act on advice, instructions, and so on that we believe in, unless we are desperate. Like any other discourse, then, a poem affects our conduct if and only if we respect what it says about the "real nature of things."

Establishing the truth of a poem, is, to be sure, difficult. Arnold was leery of trying to demonstrate the truth of a literary work partly because he relied on a simplified notion of proof indebted to the positivism of his age. In a fairly typical contribution to an 1867 collection of essays on education, J. M. Wilson maintained that science is "the *best* teacher of accurate, acute, and exhaustive observation of what is."[12] As Arnold himself suggested in the letter to Clough I have already quoted, accurately representing the world meant solving it or arriving at an unimpeachable factual account that left no room for ambiguity, a task better left to science than to poetry. Proof, in short, connoted an indisputable test that a poem could not possibly pass.

In criticizing Arnold's consequent reluctance to inspect a poem's presentation of reality, I am not suggesting that we always act on what we believe to be true, much less that our beliefs are necessarily correct. We can be impulsive, whimsical, uncertain, and wrong. Similarly, we can enjoy literature despite (or even because of) its departures from what we consider reality. Some people read science fiction or Harlequin romances in this spirit; others read *Paradise Lost* much the same way. This approach to literature, while certainly defensible, is more compatible with the use of literature for amusement or diversion than with its use as a guide to conduct. Unless we are self-destructive, we act on what we think is true. Arnold's fear of inspecting the truth of literature was at odds with the social responsibilities he hoped the study of literature would assume.[13]

Arnold, to his credit, realized that the social importance of literature is not only an intellectual matter. The same conditions that impinge on the creation of literature also affect its reception. As he wrote in his Preface to *Mixed Essays,*

> Whoever seriously occupies himself with literature will soon perceive its vital connection with other agencies. Suppose a man to be so much convinced that literature is, as indisputably it is, a powerful agency for benefiting the world and for civilizing it, such a man cannot but see that there are many obstacles preventing what is salutary in literature from gaining general admission, and from producing due effect. Undoubtedly, literature can of itself do something towards removing these obstacles, and towards making straight its own way. But it cannot do all. In other words, literature is a part of civilization; it is not the whole. (VIII, 370)

For Arnold, the chief obstacle preventing literature from "producing due effect" was inequality, especially the unfair appropriation of work and leisure, which made work brutalizing toil for the many and culture inconsequential amusement for the few.

A comment by J. D. Jump suggests why inequality mattered to Arnold:

> . . . unlike some of his immediate predecessors, Arnold was not protected by private income, personal gift, sinecure, or legacy from the

obligation of working for a living in the ordinary Philistine sense of the phrase. Because he knew it in his own life, Arnold presents in his verse the dilemma of many who in the modern world are compelled to live their lives in circumstances which fail to satisfy their natures, which distract them indeed from learning what those natures are, and which they must for their own well-being periodically elude. If Arnold's land-scapes are commonly those of a week-ender—and the Georgian poets are indeed his enfeebled successors—at least he also knew and gave utterance to that unease which drives the week-ender to the country-side.[14]

Aesthetic experience, like a weekend outing, bears the mark of the world it seems to leave behind. The special quality of the experience, its distance from the demands that occupy the rest of the week, qualifies its larger value. For the middle-class person compelled to make a living in degrading circumstances, literature seems at best a safety valve or an anodyne. Implementing the poet's insights in everyday life seems as utopian as taking up permanent residence in nature. And not everyone can afford to get away, even for a weekend. For the lower-class person, making a living tends not to curtail appre-ciation of the arts but to extinguish it. Ruskin forcefully made this point in *The Crown of Wild Olive:* "the man who has been heaving clay out of a ditch all day, or driving an express train against the north wind all night, or holding a collier's helm in a gale on a lee shore, or whirling white-hot iron at a furnace mouth, is not the same man at the end of his day, or night, as one who has been sitting in a quiet room, with everything comfortable about him."[15] The "man who has been heaving clay out of a ditch all day" may lack the time, energy, and leisure required by literature.

The efficacy of literature consequently depends on political action against the economic barriers in its way. As well as teaching the classics and writing *Essays in Criticism,* Arnold's exemplary critic-educator takes part in political activity that contributes to the classless society that culture sanctions. But because Arnold tended to locate the ori-gins of inequality in the lingering vestiges of feudalism, he endorsed political measures (like reforming archaic bequest laws) that reflected his limited analysis:

> . . . surely it is easy to see that our shortcomings in civilization are due to our inequality, or in other words, that the great inequality of classes and property, which came to us from the Middle Ages and which we maintain because we have the religion of inequality, that this constitu-

tion of things, I say, has the natural and necessary effect, under present
circumstances, of materializing our upper class, vulgarizing our mid-
dle, and brutalising our lower class. And this is to fail in civilization.
("Equality," VIII, 199)

Arnold did not see that the marketplace was generating inequities
that the eradication of feudal privileges would not touch. His political
remedies, like his theory of literature, fell short of his goals.[16]

Here, too, Arnold was a product of the age that he criticized. The
failure of the French Revolution circumscribed his politics, as it did
Coleridge's and Wordsworth's. After the Reign of Terror, revolution
forever meant absolutism, impatience, and destruction:

> Violent indignation with the past, abstract systems of renovation ap-
> plied wholesale, a new doctrine drawn up in black and white for elab-
> oration down to the very smallest details in a rational society for the
> future,—these are the ways of Jacobinism. . . . [C]ulture is the eternal
> opponent of the two things which are the signal marks of Jacobin-
> ism,—its fierceness, and its addiction to an abstract system . . . for
> Jacobinism, therefore, culture,—eternally passing onwards and seek-
> ing,—is an impertinence and an offence. (CA, 109–11)

Recoiling from the "fierceness" of Jacobinism, Arnold settled for a
well-intentioned but shortsighted attack on feudalism. His political
ideas were ineffectual, not malignant, as some radical critics have
supposed.[17] Although he saw the need for "great changes" (CA, 136),
he never found the political means of bringing them about.

It is one thing, of course, to criticize Arnold and another to remedy
the shortcomings in his work. In this chapter I have been trying to
identify the limitations of his criticism rather than overcome them.
Although I endorse Arnold's goals—in particular, equality and the
integration of culture and work—I question his means of achieving
them. Gaining "general admission" for "what is salutary in literature"
depends upon intellectual work on behalf of the truth of literature
and appropriate political action.

Instead of completing Arnold's project, as I am advocating here,
critics like Goodheart and Dickstein appeal to it as it is, thus minimizing its limits. (I say "minimizing" because while both Goodheart and
Dickstein point to flaws in Arnold—Dickstein, for example, complaining that he was out of touch with the literature of his time—

neither critic confronts the more radical problems in Arnold that I have been discussing.) Claiming to overturn Arnold, Hartman and other recent critics perpetuate the political myopia and the skepticism that make up his most dubious legacy. Rather than reinforce the inadequate underpinnings of Arnold's theory, the first group of critics speaks as if his defense of culture were secure, while the second lets it crumble.

I turn in my next chapter to Northrop Frye, a critic, like Arnold, nearly synonymous with the defense of poetry in modern criticism. (Hartman seems to me right, if unnecessarily arch, in calling Frye's "witty if understated *vision* of the critical enterprise" "the most liberal theology or justification of art the modern professional has managed to devise" [*CW,* 183–84]. In much the same spirit, Harold Bloom has called Arnold "the greatest of all school inspectors.") Although Frye has not written on deconstruction, readers have found in his work an answer to many of the questions that deconstruction raises. It seems to me, however, that Frye, like Arnold, unwittingly encourages the skepticism about literature that he tries to forestall. I should add that I am not offering here a comprehensive assessment of Frye's achievement or Arnold's, but using their work to shed light on the etiology of deconstruction, much as a physician learns about a disease by observing the remedies that fail to cure it.

II

The Imagination as a Sanction of Value: Northrop Frye and the Usefulness of Literature

Despite its fascination with categories, Northrop Frye's criticism resists categorizing because his thinking, like Coleridge's or Hegel's, is constantly in motion, starting from literature but expanding to include such larger contexts as culture and mythology. Many readers of Frye cut short the movement of his thought and lift ideas from it that seem especially fruitful or objectionable. Two Northrop Fryes have emerged from this static way of reading him. Frye the formalist extends the New Critics' attempt to claim autonomy for literature and objectivity for criticism. Instead of relating literature to politics, psychology, or history, he dispassionately charts the archetypes that literary works derive from literature as a whole, a self-sufficient, self-enclosed realm. Frye the activist, however, positions literature within culture and makes poets legislators. By keeping alive freedom and other values, poetry, in his view, informs all attempts to improve the given world.

Not surprisingly, Frye has answered that both views of him are true when we see them as successive moments in a larger argument. He makes the discontinuity of literature from life—its resistance to prose paraphrase, ethical judgment, and other forms of reduction—the source of its importance: the poet, by defying the constraints of history, religious faith, reason, and politics, stands at the center of our efforts to construct the world we desire. Despite its virtues—and they are considerable—Frye's theory cannot finally have it both ways. The importance he attaches to literature conflicts with the freedom from

14

reference that he allows it. His theory accordingly does not simply fall prey to deconstruction; it self-deconstructs, by which I mean that it sets in motion the dismantling of its most ambitious claims for literary study.

Frye has often acknowledged that his own ideas about literature extend the romantic revolution that he describes in *Fearful Symmetry, A Study of English Romanticism,* and numerous essays. Looking over his career in "The Search for Acceptable Words" (1973), he notes,

> I expected that a good deal of contemporary literature would be devoted to attacking the alleged complacency of the values and standards I had been brought up in, and was not greatly disturbed when it did. But with the rise of Hitler in Germany, the agony of the Spanish Civil War, and the massacres and deportations of Stalinism, things began to get more serious. For Eliot to announce that he was Classical in literature, royalist in politics, and Anglo-Catholic in religion was all part of the game. But the feeling of personal outrage and betrayal that I felt when I opened *After Strange Gods* was something else again. And when Eliot was accompanied by Pound's admiration for Mussolini, Yeats' flirtations with the most irresponsible of the Irish leaders, Wyndham Lewis' interest in Hitler, and the callow Marxism of younger writers, I felt that I could hardly get interested in any poet who was not closer to being the opposite in all respects to what Eliot thought he was. Or, if that was too specific, at least a poet who, even if dead, was still fighting for something that was alive.[1]

That poet, Frye goes on to say, was William Blake; the study of his work, begun in 1933, led to *Fearful Symmetry* (1947) and eventually to the theory of literature and criticism developed in the *Anatomy* (1957). The progression, Frye observes, "from one interest to the other was inevitable, and it was obvious to anyone who read both books that my critical ideas had been derived from Blake."[2]

Frye's extension of romanticism builds on his assumption that Blake's art is at its center. The romantic movement marked what Frye calls the "recovery of projection," or the discovery that all forms of civilization—institutions as well as works of art—originate in the human imagination rather than imitate prior models.[3] The advancement of science, of course, precipitated this discovery by discrediting the ascription of beauty, community, and other human values to the objective world. Although a poet like Wordsworth nevertheless sought the moral "ministry" of nature, Blake knew that the artist's freedom from preexistent reality was unconditional and the very source of civilization itself. In Frye's words,

> Blake was the first and the most radical of the Romantics who identified the creative imagination of the poet with the creative power of God. . . . Everything we call "nature," the physical world around us, is sub-moral, sub-human, sub-imaginative; every act worth performing has as its object the redeeming of this nature into something with a genuinely human, and therefore divine, shape. Hence Blake's poetry is not allegorical but mythopoeic, not obliquely related to a rational understanding of the human situation, the resolution of which is out of human hands, but a product of the creative energy that alone can redeem that situation.[4]

In Blake, the romantic "recovery of projection" found its most uncompromising advocate, a poet who refused to share his creativity with nature or derive it from a transcendent God.

Frye's own contribution to criticism in the *Anatomy* picked up where Blake left off and responded to twentieth-century critics much as Blake had reacted to his romantic contemporaries. Although critics like Cleanth Brooks, Allen Tate, and W. K. Wimsatt had exempted art from imitation of the rationally known world, they had nevertheless betrayed a Wordsworthian willingness to claim objective knowledge for art and thus qualify the artist's autonomy. Literary works, they argued, are distinct from "scientific, historical, and philosophical propositions," but they still offer us "complete knowledge of man's experience." Though not "the handmaiden of some doctrine which it is to reflect or 'communicate,'" poetry, in Brooks's words, is "far more central to man's nature than any subjective projection."[5] As Murray Krieger first pointed out in *The New Apologists for Poetry* (1956), this correspondence of poetry to reality remained nebulous, however, because no "scientific or philosophical yardstick" could measure it.[6]

Frye injected into this discussion a Blakean renunciation of all such self-contradictory attempts to fit art to an external referent. Without equivocation, he has insisted in all his works that "the writer is neither a watcher nor a dreamer. Literature does not reflect life, but it doesn't escape or withdraw from life either: it swallows it. And the imagination won't stop until it's swallowed everything."[7] He reaches this conclusion by contrasting two approaches to experience: detachment and concern. When viewed with detachment, reality appears an amoral, inalterable environment. Instead of disputing the truth of detachment, Frye, like Arnold, stresses its emotional and moral inadequacy. Emotionally, it leaves us isolated and angry, like Carlyle when he thought, "the Universe was all void of Life, of Purpose, of Volition, even of Hostility" (*Sartor Resartus*). Morally, when we are detached from what we see, we feel directionless, not knowing what to do with nature or ourselves. Politically, we feel hopeless; the world will not change or go away.

Concerned discourse expresses our dissatisfaction. If science is the language of detachment, mythology is the language of concern. Myths humanize rather than imitate reality, turning, for instance, the passage from winter to spring into a drama of death and rebirth that obviously has greater moral and emotional appeal than a weatherman's chart. Although myths violate scientific standards of truth, they nevertheless create a world that Frye can at times call "reality." "The real world," he writes, "that is, the human world, has constantly to be created, and the one model on which we must not create it is that of the world out there. The world out there has no human values, hence we should think of it primarily not as real but as absurd."[8] When we ask that myths correspond to the "world out there," we are guilty of the vice of anxiety, or the "refusal to accept the fact that man continually creates his world anew": he cannot have it "fit something outside itself."[9]

The same forces that construct myths—imagination, desire, concern—also create literary works. Myths, indeed, become literature when we cease to believe in them. Literature, like mythology, imposes form on a world that does not make human sense. "The standard of reality" for literary works consequently "does not inhere in what is there" outside themselves, "but in an unreal and subjective excess over what is there which then comes into being with its own kind of reality."[10] Desire, not truth, sanctions literary works, which respect our need for a world that is more human than a meaningless succession of facts.

Frye concedes to historical scholars that particular facts are present in literary works: hence the validity of the historical approach. But he goes on to argue that when specific references enter literary works, they transcend their referential status and become symbols. Factual errors (like Keats's mistaken reference to Cortez in his sonnet on Chapman's Homer) consequently do not matter; we are interested in something more. All efforts to hold the work accountable to some external referent are similarly misguided, whether the referent be moral universals in neoclassicism, the personal unconscious in Freud or the collective one in Jung, social history in Marx, or God in Jacques Maritain. Other critics, Frye implies, free literature from one model of imitation only to fit it to another, as Sir Philip Sidney, for instance, does when he allows for the poet's transcendence of facts but not moral precepts. Literary works for Frye, however, finally come from literature, which he pictures as a self-contained, all-inclusive universe of words that expands to swallow all realities ouside itself. The circumference of literature is nowhere, or rather, at the limits of our boundless desire; its center is any literary work.

Frye's disarming references to texts that many of us have never heard of, much less read, unintentionally create the impression that he surveys literature from above, like a god overseeing his creation. But Frye assumes that literature is a self-contained universe; by his own admission he never demonstrates it. To be sure, some works, like the apocalyptic late works of Blake, Joyce, and others, suggest an imagination capable of containing everything. But the self-enclosed wholeness of literature is not a verifiable conclusion but a supposition that Frye has to make if he is to prevent literary works from escaping to an outer world that may cause or explain them. No critic is less eager to justify literature in terms of its correspondence to reality.

Except maybe Oscar Wilde: Frye's central claim that literature shapes itself and is consequently not to be judged in terms of its truth to any external model recalls many similar statements in *Intentions.* In *The Secular Scripture* Frye accordingly approves of Wilde's dictum that literature is "always a form of 'lying,' that is, of turning away from the descriptive use of language and the correspondence form of truth."[11] In *Creation and Recreation,* after restating the view that "mythology is the embryo of literature and the arts, not of science, and no form of art has anything to do with making direct statements about nature, mistaken or correct," Frye again concludes,

> All this is contained in Wilde's conception of the creative arts as essentially forms of 'lying,' or turning away from the external world. As long as we can keep telling one another that we see the same things 'out there,' we feel that we have a basis for what we call truth and reality. When a work of literature is based on this kind of reality, however, it often tells us only what we no longer want to know. . . . What Wilde calls realism, the attempt to base the arts on the recognizable, to find a

common ground of reality with the audience, is, he suggests, a search for some kind of emotional reassurance.[12]

But whereas Wilde made literature an end in itself, Frye, as I noted at the outset, wants to defend its larger usefulness. A desire to protect art, not to change society, motivated Wilde's commitment to literary autonomy. "In a very ugly and sensible age," he wrote in *Intentions,* "the arts borrow, not from life, but from each other,"[13] but they do so to keep themselves pure, not to remake the world that repulses them. Frye, by contrast, frees literature from history not only for its own sake but for the sake of human freedom:

> The ethical purpose of a liberal education is to liberate, which can only mean to make one capable of conceiving society as free, classless, and urbane. No such society exists, which is one reason why a liberal education must be deeply concerned with works of imagination. The imaginative element in works of art, again, lifts them clear of the bondage of history. . . . Thus liberal education liberates the works of culture themselves as well as the mind they educate.[14]

Although literature makes no assertions, in its very freedom from reference it presumably checks our advancement toward a "self-policing state," or a society "incapable of formulating an articulate criticism of itself and of developing a will to act in its light."[15]

Literature, in short, sanctions a vision of an egalitarian, liberated society that indicts the repression, division, and hopelessness we see all around us. In *Creation and Recreation,* after applauding Wilde's equation of art with lying, Frye accordingly goes on to say,

> What we see continually in the world around us is a constant and steady perversion of the vision of a free and equal social future, as country after country makes a bid for freedom and accepts instead a tyranny far worse than the one it endured before. . . . [T]he arts actually represent an immense imaginative and transforming force in society, which is largely untapped because so much of our approach to them is still possessive and aesthetic. There is a much deeper level on which the arts form part of our heritage of freedom, and where inner repression by the individual and external repression in society make themselves constantly felt. That is why totalitarian societies, for example, find themselves unable either to tolerate the arts or to generate new forms of them. During the Nazi occupation of France, the French discovered that one of the most effective things they could do was to put on classical plays like *Antigone* or *The Trojan Woman,* in original or

adapted versions. The Nazis had no excuse for censoring them, but because of the intense repression all around, the plays began to mean something of what they really do mean.

Literary works can be weapons against oppression, not simply objects "to be admired or valued or possessed," objects of "the sort indicated by Wilde's term 'beautiful.' "[16]

In Frye's view, oppression occurs in societies that have forgotten that they have created their values, in Frye's parlance, their "myths of concern." Anxious to perpetrate an established order that benefits them, elites in particular fail to remember that their myths of concern are myths. Like the priests in Blake's *Marriage of Heaven and Hell,* they turn poetic tales into forms of worship and facts of nature. What they have only created, they think they have proved or discovered. Efforts to change society betray the same self-serving forgetfulness as efforts to keep it as it is. "Revolutionary action, of whatever kind," Frye observes in the *Anatomy,* "leads to the dictatorship of one class, and the record of history seems clear that there is no quicker way of destroying the benefits of culture."[17] The revolutionary pursuit of liberty inevitably turns into the reign of more or less obvious terror, just as transitional periods of repression have a way of lasting forever. Society, in short, seems an "eternally unwilling recipient of culture."[18]

By "culture," Frye, then, means not "one more objective environment" but the indispensable power of conceiving more desirable alternatives to our present one.[19] We derive this power not so much from an individual literary work as from the totality of our literary experience, which frees us by dissolving apparent necessity into possibility. Despite our political efforts, life in society can never free us so completely as the imagination.

> The only genuine freedom is a freedom of the will which is informed by a vision, and this vision can only come to us through the intellect and the imagination, and through the arts and sciences which embody them, the analogies of whatever truth and beauty we can reach. In this kind of freedom the opposition to necessity disappears: for scientists and artists and scholars, as such, what they want to do and what they have to do become the same thing. This is the core of freedom that no concern can ever include or replace, and everything else that we associate with freedom proceeds from it.[20]

Romance, for Frye the heart of literature, illustrates this view of freedom in its very structure. Unlike comedy, which terminates in a new community, romance "has no continuing city as its final resting place": "We reach the ideal of romance through a progressive bursting of closed circles, first of social mythology, whether frivolous or serious, then of nature, and finally of the comic-providential universe of Christianity and other religions, including Marxism, which contains them both" ("social mythology" is Frye's term for the established values of our social environment).[21]

Frye's lifelong allegiance to the university follows from his assumption that imaginative experience constitutes the foundation of freedom upon which everything else more or less inadequately builds. The university, in fact, provides "the only visible direction in which our higher loyalties and obligations can go," because it keeps alive "the freedom that comes only from articulateness, the ability to produce, as well as respond, to verbal structures."[22] Frye is not naïve; he realizes that the university can be as competitive, quantitative, and unfair as the world outside. But despite its imperfections, this institution, more than any other, preserves access to the "articulated worlds of consciousness, the intelligible and imaginative worlds, that are at once the reward of freedom and the guarantee of it."[23] His defense of literature, like Arnold's, ends in a defense of the university, whose autonomy he justifies in the name of human freedom, not out of concern for the careers of a few teachers and scholars.

Frye's defense of literature is attractive in many ways. Despite the compulsions that distort teaching and criticism today, it is true that for many scholars and teachers, "what they want to do and what they have to do" are one. Frye's awareness of what might be called, for lack of a better word, the joys of criticism has made him especially sensitive to the disappointments of younger scholars:

> Like other older academics, I spend a lot of time writing letters of recommendation for jobs, promotions, and tenure appointments, and I get a strong impression that not only the administration but the senior teaching staff in many universities will snatch at almost any excuse to deny these things. . . . [N]o scholar is an island; everyone's scholarly fortunes are inseparable from those of one's colleagues and of the profession as a whole. Students emerging from graduate school with a genuine vocation and commitment are a part of my own scholarly life, and their frustrations and humiliations frustrate and humiliate me also.[24]

Here, and throughout his criticism, Frye affirms community, generosity, and fairness, values that some other recent theorists (Harold Bloom, for instance) have deemed idealizations. Frye's effort to align literary study with these ends seems to me appropriate but disappointing, for reasons that help us understand the subsequent unraveling of his claims.

The loose thread in Frye's system is his relativistic theory of value, described at greatest length in *The Critical Path.*

> Evidently we must come to terms with the fact that mythical and logical languages are distinct. The vision of things as they could or should be certainly has to depend on the vision of things as they are. But what is between them is not so much a point of contact as an existential gap, a revolutionary and transforming act of choice. The beliefs we hold and the kind of society we try to construct are chosen from infinite possibilities, and the notion that our choices are inevitably connected with things as they are, whether through the mind of God or the constitution of nature, always turns out to be an illusion of habit.[25]

If it is impossible to live objectively (because "things as they are" can never sanction our vision of what we ought to do), it is also dangerous to live mythically. Disregarding reason, in other words, is as undesirable as abiding exclusively by it. When we protect our beliefs and values from reason, Frye suggests, we tend toward fanaticism, bigotry, censorship, superstition, and other closed positions. We lock ourselves in ideas that other people can betray, threaten, and absorb, but never correct.

Instead of opting for either concern or detachment, Frye is arguing, then, for an endless tension between the two. Objective criticism saves a myth of concern from stasis and intolerance, while desire legitimizes our choice to value anything, even the knowledge of non-mythical realities. The study of literature—in Frye's terms, the detached, scientific examination of concerned discourse—teaches us that our own concerns are possibilities, not imperatives described in fact. Such a discovery, in Frye's view, opens our minds as well as our concerns, thus justifying the ambitious pronouncements on behalf of literature noted repeatedly throughout this chapter (that "the arts form part of our heritage of freedom," and so on).

Frye's respect for reason is clear, but, for all his deference to things as they are, values in his theory are finally arbitrary. External reality validates none of our myths of concern, and the imagination sanctions all of them. An indemonstrable "transforming act of choice" consequently makes us prefer *The Four Zoas* over *Mein Kampf,* even democracy over tyranny. For Frye, the subjective status of values frees us from society's norms by allowing us to see that society's myths of concern are only myths. He does not acknowledge, however, that the same logic undercuts his own position. If submission to established authority is a purely personal choice, then so is opposition. Although Frye's relativism may inspire the critical attitude toward society that he values, it may also legitimize the passivity that he deplores—the paralysis that cripples John Barth's heroes, for example, when they find that everything is possible but nothing is rationally defensible, or, more to the point of my argument here, the disillusionment with progress that informs deconstruction. Frye's argument, in short, defeats itself. The weapon he turns against his adversaries' values—the subjectivity of all values—undermines his own, reducing even his esteem for literature to a rationally indefensible preference.

Objections to the criticisms I am making here take the following well-worn form: No approach to values can avoid the weakness I have attributed to Frye's. Even when we base equality or democracy, say, in human nature, the mind of God, or some other ostensibly external realm, we do not guarantee these values or make them indisputably clear. People have used "human nature" to shore up all kinds of horrors (like slavery); as a guide to values it is no more firm or selective than the autonomous imagination. The only way, in fact, to support values in the way I apparently desire is through censorship, indoctrination, or some other totalitarian means of insuring compliance with them. The great virtue of Frye's theory is that he lets us choose our myths of concern.

Indeed (in some versions of this argument) totalitarianism necessarily results from claiming objective truth for one's point of view. Michel Foucault makes this point in his influential "Discourse on Language": the "will to truth" ultimately masks a will to power. Our feeling that we are right—that the "discursive formation" we inhabit reflects things as they are—moves us to punish, ostracize, and otherwise correct those who err, like parents spanking children or psychiatrists branding patients insane. Claiming truth for one's norms means privileging them and more or less violently imposing them on those who disagree.

This equation between relativism and tolerance—axiomatic in

much recent criticism—seems to me misleading. In more convincing defenses of tolerance—John Stuart Mill's *On Liberty,* for example—we respect the views of others because we think we may be able to learn from them. We suppose, in other words, that we are talking about something, or, more precisely, about the same things; one person's opinion can accordingly correct, support, and in other ways contribute to another's. Far from cutting off dialogue, belief in the possibility of objective truth allows discussion to take place. We cannot logically claim that we are right without holding out the possibility that we are wrong—the possibility that keeps us talking and listening. Tyrants who liquidate their adversaries and teachers who abuse their students are not rational or objective but illogical—in love more with power than with the complex truth.

Frye, of course, is not advocating authoritarianism, but, by making principled agreement about values impossible, he would seem to make some recourse to force inevitable. A society cannot exist without affirming some values at the expense of others, and Frye gives us no rational way of making or protesting that choice (which is perhaps why he finds freedom in "articulateness," not in politics or public life). Historically, as Gerald Graff has shown, the literature of fascism abounds with assertions that "all ideologies are merely fictions" (as Mussolini put it): " 'might makes right' is no less logical a deduction" than tolerance from the premise that all myths of concern are fictions.[26] If all rules are arbitrary, I am suggesting, might must make right. Nothing else can. Instead of constituting a problem, the rule of force becomes a necessity.

Frye's relativism, in short, threatens the defense of literature that he calls on it to guarantee. In Frye's view, literature is worthwhile—in fact, irreplaceable—because it alone safeguards tolerance, personal freedom, and untrammeled discussion, all the values that open a society and its "mythology." Like Frye, I endorse these values and agree that they result when we look at our value judgments with detachment, seeing them as possibilities open to confirmation, correction, or refutation. In my view, however, the belief that we may be wrong inspires us to heed other points of view. In Frye's theory, because we cannot be right about value judgments, we need not suppose that we can be wrong. Being right, whether about politics or the value of literature, drops out as an incentive to dialogue. In the absence of any way of testing the truth of ethical judgments, debate about them collapses into the power struggle that Frye wants literature to combat.

I have been describing what we must come to terms with if, as Frye maintains, norms can have no basis in reason or fact. Instead of arguing that "mythical and logical languages are distinct," Frye asserts it, pointing to Thomism and Marxism as examples of "closed mythologies" that pretend to ground norms in things as they are with disastrous results. When Thomists and Marxists claim to satisfy the tests of reason and history, they slant the "evidence" in their favor, shackling reason to faith in the one instance and rewriting history in the other. They construct an untenable "deductive synthesis" in which knowledge loses its autonomy to some kind of social authority: a church or a political party, a pope or a commissar. What is, again, can never underwrite what should be.

These examples do not constitute an argument. As numerous philosophers have recently contended, we may be able to give reasons for ethical and aesthetic judgments without falling back on whimsical metaphysical assumptions.[27] Frye implies that either we base values in some transcendental realm (God, for example) or we declare them groundless. But there are more persuasive intermediate positions that he ignores. Concentrating on Thomism and Marxism—and a crude version of Marxism at that—is like judging the novel by *Love Story*. What for Frye is a settled matter—the separation of facts from values—is today an open question, at least among many philosophers.

It was also an open question among the English romantics, whom Frye so eloquently champions. Despite his formidable skill in interpreting these poets, he lacks sympathy with the quest for moral authority that inspired their major poetry. For Frye, as for some existentialists, when we try to authenticate values by reference to the "world out there," we commit the "vice of anxiety," betray an almost pathetic need for "emotional reassurance," and refuse "to accept the fact that man continually creates his world anew." Even if these needs motivate the quest for objective values—and I am not sure that they do—they do not prove that quest wrong. Wordsworth, for one, really believed that he found

> In nature and the language of the sense
> The anchor of [his] purest thoughts, the nurse
> The guide, the guardian of [his] heart, and soul
> Of all [his] moral being.
>
> ("Tintern Abbey," ll. 108–11)

Even Blake claimed reality for his values, not, to be sure, the reality of

natural objects but the reality of "Mental Things," which "are alone
Real." For him, the imagination is "the true faculty of knowing" and
"Vision" is the "Representation of what Eternally Exists, Really &
Unchangeably."[28] As I have shown elsewhere, these cognitive claims
are admittedly more complex than they first appear.[29] But Frye has no
room for them, however complicated, in his theory. At best, they are
mistakes; at worst, they are delusions born of nervousness and fear.

I realize that I have not remedied the difficulties that, in my opinion, result from Frye's elision of the romantics' cognitive claims for
literature. Appealing to the undesirable consequences of a position
does not invalidate it, just as calling the fact-value dichotomy an open
question among contemporary philosophers and the English romantics hardly bridges the gap between fact and value. I think, however,
that we can heal the split between these two terms, along lines that
Frye makes available but never pursues. Even as Frye's theory creates
problems for itself, it also points to a way out of them.

This way out appears when Frye concedes that the norms heeded
by the detached observer—evidence, logic, and so on—are approxi-
mations, making objective (i.e., absolutely certain, unmediated) truth
impossible to obtain or verify. Similarly, he adds, every verbal structure "contains mythical and fictional features simply because it is a
verbal structure,"[30] shaped by the "conditions of grammar" and, in
some instances, "the demands of narrative," not simply copied from
the object it studies. Unlike deconstructionist critics and some writers
who have been influenced by his work (Hayden White, for instance, in
Metahistory), Frye goes on to conclude that the "mythical and fictional
features" of discourse complicate objective knowledge rather than
eliminate it. However elusive, truth of correspondence remains for
him an important procedural ideal; chastened by our awareness of
the difficulties that attend such a claim, we can still say we have access
to things as they are.

It seems to me that Frye's defense of the truth of detachment ought
also to apply to literature. I see no reason why, if the "demands of
narrative" and "the conditions of grammar" leave standing the
referentiality of extraliterary discourse, they neverthelesss annul the
referentiality of literature. Having kept open the possibility of reference elsewhere, Frye inexplicably seals it shut in his dealings with
literary texts. I am working here toward one of the intermediate

positions in ethics and literary theory that I earlier chastised Frye for overlooking. I join ethics and literary theory because of the logical connection between them, not just in Frye's criticism but in critical theory generally. In Frye, a subjectivist theory of value leads to, even necessitates, a nonreferential view of literature. Because Frye confines knowledge to facts, he cannot count as knowledge concerned (i.e., value-laden) discourse like literature.

In the theory that I am broaching here, literary works, by contrast, offer neither imaginative possibilities for us to contemplate nor infallible propositions for us to take on faith, but admittedly normative statements about the world that we can act on, debate, and judge. Obviously much more needs to be said on behalf of such a theory of literature (beyond complaining about Frye's hasty dismissal of it).[31] Here, however, I want again to emphasize the cost of rejecting it. By denying that evaluative assertions can be true to things as they are, Frye defends literary study on grounds that make it rationally indefensible.

I suggested earlier that opposing fact to value is a common move in contemporary literary theory. To give some support to this claim, I want to conclude this chapter by briefly looking at Frank Kermode's influential study in the theory of fiction, *The Sense of an Ending* (1967). In addition to highlighting some similarities between Frye and another major twentieth-century critic, I hope to bring into sharper focus the implications of the separation of literature from knowledge that I have been analyzing in the work of Frye and Arnold.

The Sense of an Ending tells a story that students of romantic and postromantic literature have often heard before. In the past (Kermode does not say when), we believed in our fictions, or, what is the same thing, we did not think of them as fictions. We gave them "absolute assent." We thought that the world made sense, that history in particular had a plot or shape to it that our narratives (the Bible, for example) could imitate. Sometime, somehow (again Kermode does not say), we became "sophisticated." We skeptically rejected our earlier trust in fictions as "naïve." We discovered that the world lacks meaning, a beginning, and an end, and that history is a flux of arbitrary, senseless events.

I have already mentioned Frye's more complex version of this story in *A Study in English Romanticism*. Like Frye, Kermode goes on to argue that despite our newly acquired knowledge, we still retain our need for fictions. We cannot live in the cold, "hostile world" without the consoling sense of direction, purpose, and coherence that fictions afford. So we hold onto our fictions, while self-consciously seeing them as fictions. We give them "conditional" or "experimental" assent, using them as long as they are not too false to reality. When they are wrong, we either abandon or sophisticate them (as Joyce refines Homer, say, or Pynchon complicates the myth of the Holy Grail). To stay "effective," literature changes with our understanding of reality without, of course, ceasing to impose form on a formless world.

As my cursory summary should indicate, Kermode uses "fiction" and "literature" indiscriminately. More accurately, he subsumes literary works under the broader category of anything that orders the preexistent world. Any narrative, whether a history or a personal anecdote, is fictive to the extent that it arranges events in a coherent sequence. For Kermode, arranging events means manipulating them, wrenching them into a pattern that they do not in reality follow. In his usage, "fictive" consequently means false (i.e., not true to anything external). Sometimes he goes so far as to suggest that all accounts of reality are fictive, even supposedly objective or scientific ones, in which case we adjust our narratives to what we call "reality," not to reality itself. But more often, like Frye, he speaks as if objective knowledge were possible. Without referring to reality, he cannot explain why literature changes or why fictions are fictions.

A curious mixture of compliance and resistance accordingly defines Kermode's argument. While he complies with the "sophisticated" view that fictions are false, he nevertheless resists getting rid of them. Again, even though fictions are falsehoods, we should not—we cannot—dispense with them.

> We need ends and *kairoi* and the *pleroma*, even now when the history of the world has so terribly and so untidily expanded its endless succes-siveness. We re-create the horizons we have abolished, the structures that have collapsed; and we do so in terms of the old patterns, adapting them to our new worlds. . . . For concord or consonance really is the root of the matter, even in a world which thinks it can only be a fiction.[32]

What seems at first an attack on literature (it is "only" fiction) ends up an argument for literature ("even now" we need it).

When Kermode tries to discriminate among fictions, however, his argument, like Frye's, breaks down. Although Kermode wants to say that knowledge of reality dictates our response to fictions, he never specifies when fictions become too incredible to retain their "operational effectiveness"—when some deviation from reality becomes too much. He cannot draw this line because he cannot say why, if we recognize fictions as fictions, we should care about their compliance with the real world. As I argued in my last chapter, if we want to defend the effectiveness of literature—one of Kermode's aims—then any deviation from reality would seem too much, unless, of course, we hold that there is no such thing as reality. Without believing in astrology, for example, I may enjoy consulting my horoscope, but when faced with a decision about an operation I will ask a doctor, if I believe in medicine and if I value my life. (I may stick with my horoscope—or flip a coin—if the decision is trivial and/or no pertinent knowledge is available.) We are affected as we believe, Samuel Johnson often maintained, making an empirical point about human behavior that I take to be true. By labeling literary works "fictions," Kermode curtails the "operational effectiveness" he seeks to uphold.

Sometimes he seems aware of the limited importance he is giving literature. "What Vaihinger calls 'reunion with reality,'" he says at one point, "and I call 'making sense' or 'making human sense' is something that literature achieves only so long as we remember the status of fictions. They are not myths, and they are not hypotheses; you neither arrange the world to suit them, nor test them by experiment, for instance in gas-chambers."[33] Unlike myths (which we believe), fictions are in practical terms innocuous, lacking any decisive impact on the way we arrange the world. When earlier thinkers believed in fictions—when they consequently ordered their lives by them—Kermode concedes that these thinkers "took fictions seriously."[34] We, by implication, do not.

In these first two chapters I have been preparing for my critique of deconstruction by plumbing the theory's origins. I use "origins" here in a logical rather than a historical sense.[35] A history of deconstruction would begin with a thinker like Nietzsche, say, who welcomes deconstruction, not with critics like Frye and Arnold, who try to resist it. I have nevertheless concentrated on Arnold and Frye because they do not simply oppose deconstruction; they also initiate it by distrusting the cognitive credentials of the literary works that they seek to defend. (I should add that this distrust of literature is one of deconstruction's starting points, but not the only one.)

A passage from *Creation and Recreation* captures the treacherous position in which Arnold, Frye, and, I have argued, Kermode leave the study of literature:

> In the nineteenth century we see that the mythological picture which survived Dante for many centuries has finally and totally changed. There is no longer any functional place for a divine creation at the beginning of things: there is only human culture, and therefore at most only the sense of human recreation as a distant goal. But human culture and its goals are not guaranteed by anything like a universe of law rooted in the nature of God himself, much less by any will on the part of a God to redeem. On the contrary, they are guaranteed by nothing and are threatened by practically everything. Everywhere we turn in the nineteenth century, we find a construct reminding us of a Noah's ark bearing the whole surviving life of a world struggling to keep afloat in a universal storm.[36]

Despite the confidence of these critics in the value of literary study, for them, too, literature is a "Noah's ark," its authority jeopardized by the neutralization of knowledge, or the constriction of reason to fact (which reduces the insights of literary works to fictions in Kermode, vague "ideas" in Arnold, and imaginative possibilities in Frye); the bankruptcy of politics, its dwindling into a "specialized chess game" that only perpetuates repression (which limits the influence of literature to acts of consciousness that no "continuing city" can realize); and a hostile society, "eternally unwilling" to benefit from culture (which keeps literature in the university, off the streets, and out of the workplace). "Threatened by practically everything," literature is "guaranteed by nothing," the fictiveness of all values having undermined the legitimacy of these critics' own values, making their respect for literary works an arbitrary, rationally indefensible choice.

Literature, to be sure, does make a positive difference to human life in these theories: without it, things would be even worse. By keeping the storm at bay, literature checks what it cannot stop—"the constant and steady perversion of the vision of a free and equal social future," which "we see continually in the world around us."

Instead of solving the problems that I find in this criticism, I have tried to identify them, arguing that a narrow view of knowledge and a pessimistic or shortsighted outlook on politics combine to undercut the cognitive authority of literature and to diminish, if not eliminate, its practical importance. Inheriting the problem of the marginality of literature, deconstruction tries to solve it, not, however, by expanding knowledge to include literature or by constructing a politics of equality and freedom, as I have been advocating, but by infecting both knowledge and politics with what deconstructionists see as the self-nullifying groundlessness of literary works. Frye's ark, already in trouble, sinks.

III

Poststructuralist Critical Theory:
Jacques Derrida, Stanley Fish,
and J. Hillis Miller

As my preceding chapters suggest, when poststructuralist critics dismantle the truth of literature, they knock down a structure that is already falling. This fact partly explains what I take to be the most significant feature of poststructuralist criticism—the disparity between its rhetoric and its impact, especially on the academic profession. The risk, anguish, and violence that these writers think accompany their work are at odds with what they are actually doing, which is to accelerate developments that have been going on without them. It is no accident that deconstruction in particular first caught on at some of our most renowned universities, or that individuals thoroughly at home in the academic profession have switched their loyalty from Wimsatt or Frye to Jacques Derrida. Neither does the ease with which the university has assimilated deconstruction prove its capacity for tolerating dangerous ideas. The ideas themselves are not dangerous.[1]

In my next two chapters I look at several contemporary critics, some of them deconstructionists (Paul de Man, Jacques Derrida, J. Hillis Miller, Tilottama Rajan), some of them not (Harold Bloom, Stanley Fish). All of these critics, however, argue for the indeterminacy of literary texts, although they define "indeterminacy" in different ways. I focus on the question of indeterminacy because of its importance not only to the theory of interpretation but also to the poststructuralist attack on academic criticism. In chapter 5 I criticize the stasis that results when poststructuralists use the putative undecidability of texts as a weapon against academic literary study. But before arguing that the claim of indeterminacy is costly, I want first to show that it is unjustified—unjustified, that is, by the incoherent arguments that try to advance it and the unsatisfying readings that depend on it.

By deconstruction I mean a view of literature derived from Jacques Derrida's theory of writing and, more distantly, from the linguistics of Ferdinand de Saussure. Derrida's assumptions about writing are by now well known, but his argument in support of them needs mentioning, in part because it is taken for granted by some American literary critics influenced by his work. Writing, in his view, is less a vehicle of communication or knowledge than an independent force that renders "problematic" whatever message we try to get across by means of it. Even the simplest forms of writing—a note, say, conveying information—is like the most involuted literary work: self-complicating and indecipherable. A text, to be sure, always seems on the verge of becoming whole, intelligible, and coherent. But the sign we hope will complete or ground it ends up deepening its complexity, functioning less as the text's center or origin than as another turn in its labyrinth. Texts, in short, are heterogeneous: they make, then erase, assertions; they begin and end arbitrarily.

In "Force and Signification" Derrida calls the infinite regress of signifiers the anguish of language: "all possible meanings push each other" against "the necessarily restricted passageway of speech," "preventing each other's emergence," yet "calling upon each other, provoking each other too, unforeseeably and as if despite oneself, in a kind of autonomous overassemblage of meanings, a power of pure equivocality that makes the creativity of the classical God appear all too poor."[2] Elsewhere, especially in "Structure, Sign, and Play," he aligns the indeterminacy of writing with joy and play, "the affirmation of a world of signs without fault, without truth, and without origin which is offered to an active interpretation."[3]

Derrida has coined a number of terms to show how a text escapes what he sees as the constraints of logic, reference, and authorial intent. "Supplementarity," for instance, describes how one sign seems to add something to its predecessors, extending (supplementing) the meaning to which the text as a whole aspires. Paradoxically, the very need for a supplement testifies to a lack or absence in what has gone before. And the sign that makes up this deficiency is itself inadequate, its truth and clarity depending on additional supplements that also turn out to be lacking. What seems at first glance purposive and cumulative—one positive term adding to (supplementing) another—

ends up going nowhere (or everywhere). Similarly, "trace" for Derrida has the common-sense meaning of a mark, track, or inscription presumably left by something. In writing, the sign (or text as a whole) traces other traces: its origin is "always already" absent. Instead of the thing itself, we find more figures that ostensibly stand for it; instead of the speaker, we discover more messages. Finally, *différance* combines differing and deferring. Signs differ from each other and, in fact, as Saussure observed, become meaningful through their differences, which often take the form of oppositions (nature, for instance, is not culture, and a red light signals stop when a green one signals go). In each instance the connection between signifier (red, for instance) and signified (stop) is arbitrary or, what is the same thing for Derrida, conventional, established by a local system of distinctions. Signifiers, in short, differ from each other and from what they signify; in Derrida's analysis, the very differences that make them meaningful keep them from meaning anything definite, much less from pointing outside themselves to an external referent. "Red" never sheds the multiple meanings it has acquired in different contexts (cities, literary works, religions, etc.), meanings that entangle it with an unlimited number of other signs and strangle its claims of reference. A word differs each time we use it, yet retains the trace(s) of its other uses. When we write, then, we multiply differences and defer the extratextual presence and clarity we are trying to attain.

Derrida uses terms like *différance* to defeat and yet at the same time to account for the distinctions of traditional logic. Writing is inherently double: it does not so much militate against presence as generate a desire for presence that it undermines. Traces, differences, supplements, signs in general, all assume the status of agents in Derrida's thought. They tempt us into picturing some reality outside themselves, but the picture is finally another sign, trace, or text that perpetuates the chain that it promises to end. The margins around a text, like the blank spaces between its letters and words, inspire the longing for something there, yet render arbitrary whatever appears. A typical Derridean reading seizes on those moments in a text when language gets the better of what an author apparently wants to say. Sometimes a single word undoes a seemingly straightforward assertion (usually a distinction), as when Rousseau says that writing "serves only as a supplement to speech" or when Wayne Booth remarks that the deconstructionist reading of a literary work "is plainly and simply parasitical" on the "obvious or univocal meaning." "Supplement" points to a "deficiency and infirmity" in speech that Rousseau fails to see; "parasitical" blurs the boundaries that Booth wants to keep intact.[4] Often a succession of figures in a text indicates the inadequacy of each one and, ultimately, the domination of authorial intent by language. In Paul de Man's reading of *The Triumph of Life*, to be discussed in my next chapter, one metaphor gives way to another not because Shelley wants it that way but because an arbitrary act of language posits and erases each one. Even purportedly deconstructive texts—Heidegger on Nietzsche, say, or Lévi-Strauss on myth—succumb to their own kind of blindness. After using the incest taboo to question the opposition of nature to culture, Lévi-Strauss, for example, still idealizes speech and suggests that writing introduces artificial divisions into communities that are "naturally" whole. These examples do not indicate contradictions that we can avoid: writing lulls us into affirmations that writing itself makes untenable.

Derrida, of course, does not exempt his own writing from the unevenness he attributes to the texts of others. We have only one language, he repeatedly says—the language of metaphysics. Even skeptics have to rely on concepts (nature, origin, intention, center, etc.) whose truth value they suspect. We cannot deconstruct origins without using the term, which trails the system of oppositions that gives it meaning. Instead of abandoning such concepts, Derrida uses them self-consciously. He vigilantly watches over his own text, checking its lapses into straightforward assertion. His puns, etymologies, and neologisms remind us how much is in one of his words—more than even he knows and more than we can pin down in a paraphrase. Numerous allusions to other texts dissolve the identity of his own, if indeed we can call such a text "his." As I have just done, he puts words in quotation marks and under erasure to show that he questions their reference. His sentence fragments and omission of transitions force us to reread what we thought we understood. When we come across

> For there could be no history without the gravity and labor of literality. The painful folding of itself which permits history to reflect itself as it ciphers itself.[5]

our effort to make sense of the text in a linear way breaks down. The fragments deflect our attention to previous sentences, where we look (vainly) for a foothold that will allow us to start again. In his anxiety to

avoid assertions of presence, Derrida in general shuns clear connections between subjects and verbs, often interrupting a sentence with
an interminable parenthetical break, itself compounded of several
clauses that circle a point rather than progress. Instead of growing
clearer, his writing, in short, thickens and folds back on itself. He
wants us to see the medium we pretend to see through. Like any other
discourse, his "risks *making sense,* risks agreeing to the reasonableness
of reason, of philosophy. . . ." But Derrida tries to "redouble language
and have recourse to ruses, to stratagems, to simulacra," to bring out
the qualities in writing that subvert its claim to make sense.[6]

If writing is so duplicitous, one wonders why he has to go to all that
trouble. If he can find indeterminacy in a statement like "I forgot my
umbrella," why does he have to strain to make his own writing so
abstruse? The answer would seem to be that he finds writing seduc-
tive. When we write, he implies, writing tempts us to believe that we
are saying something determinate. Although that belief is finally an
illusion that writing itself undercuts, it is a powerful illusion nonetheless, reinforced by legal, educational, and political systems that want
us to trust their texts. Always on guard against his own susceptibility
to assertion, Derrida plays the game of interpretation—quoting passages, citing other commentaries, arguing a thesis, and so forth—yet
he tries to show that it is just a game whose outcome is never truth to
anything outside itself.[7] For all his antinomian rhetoric, his enterprise
is finally conservative.[8] He mocks the game he is playing but he plays it
nevertheless. With respect to his readers, he stimulates the activities
that he parodies. No passage from his work stands alone; his prose
cries out for decoding, often in the most esoteric terms. A writer like
Derrida is not born but made—in the libraries, graduate schools, and
professional associations whose assumptions about texts he derides.

I will return in chapter 5 to the conservative implications of Derrida's views. ("Conservative" is an admittedly misleading term that I
will be trying to clarify.) But first we should look more closely at why
he thinks that writing is "undecidable." His argument hinges on the
arbitrariness and iterability of the sign, that is, its capacity to be used
repeatedly. I have already said that in his view the connection between
the signifier and the signified is arbitrary; so are the rules we obey
when we make sentences, essays, and literary works. Whatever we
write, moreover, must function in our absence. This chapter, for instance, has to make its own way in the world and confront diverse

readers whose presuppositions and circumstances I obviously cannot anticipate. There is nothing in my text to stop these readers from misunderstanding it. My absence from the text, for instance, eliminates my control over it and prevents me from assessing the uses others make of it. Similarly, I cannot object that readers ignore the context of what I say: imprisoned in their own culture-bound codes, they cannot comprehend my own. And the context of a text is never clear:

> As far as the internal semiotic context is concerned, the force of rupture is no less important: by virtue of its essential iterability, a written syntagma can always be detached from the chain in which it is inserted or given without causing it to lose all possibility of functioning, if not all possibility of "communicating," precisely. One can perhaps come to recognize other possibilities in it by inscribing it or *grafting* it onto other chains. No context can entirely enclose it. Nor any code, the code here being both the possibility and impossibility of writing, of its essential iterability (repetition/alterity).[9]

Even if we can identify the chain (context) in which a sign is inserted—and Derrida most often declares we cannot—its command over the parts it links is slight. Taken out of context, a sign still functions; it "loses" what it never had—the "possibility of 'communicating'" precisely. Finally, the referent I may be writing about is also missing from my text. Whether I am analyzing *Crime and Punishment,* leaving a message, or making a shopping list, no clear original, no model of imitation, can clarify what I am trying to say. My essay obviously is not *Crime and Punishment*—and what is *Crime and Punishment* but another undecidable text?

Because a text differs from what it seems to be about and because the authority of the author and context is so shaky, the possibility of misinterpretation is intrinsic to writing. In "Signature Event Context" Derrida ties misunderstanding to the very "spacing [*espacement*] that constitutes the written sign":

> spacing which separates it from other elements of the internal contextual chain (the always open possibility of its disengagement and graft), but also from all forms of present reference (whether past or future in the modified form of the present that is past or to come), objective or subjective. This spacing is not the simple negativity of a lacuna but rather the emergence of the mark. . . . This structural possibility of being weaned from the referent or from the signified (hence from

communication and from its context) seems to me to make every mark, including those which are oral, a grapheme in general; which is to say, as we have seen, the non-present *remainder [restance]* of a differential mark cut off from its putative "production" or origin. ("SEC," 182–83)

The writer, the putative origin, stands helplessly by while others graft "his" comments on texts that are never their own. Context, intent, and even syntax are so many fragile containers that the force of language bursts, endlessly dispersing the meanings of any statement, forever deferring the absolute fixing of what the statement says.

Derrida is not saying that we should abandon interpretation or categories like intention and context. Deconstruction is not destruction and Derrida's message is not "anything goes" (despite the fears of some of his adversaries and the hopes of some of his friends). Interpretation is a practical necessity, and when we make sense of an utterance, we cannot say anything we like.

Every sign, linguistic or non-linguistic, spoken or written (in the current sense of this opposition), in a small or large unit, can be *cited*, put between quotation marks; in so doing it can break with every context, engendering an infinity of new contexts in a manner which is absolutely illimitable. This does not imply that the mark is valid outside of a context, but on the contrary that there are only contexts without any center or absolute anchoring [*ancrage*]. ("SEC," 185–86)

Because Derrida situates interpretation in contexts that limit it, a Derridean interpretation does not run wild: it begins at one point rather than another, says some things instead of others. But these choices, however necessary, are finally arbitrary, lacking "any center or absolute anchoring" in the text. I close my interpretation because of a publisher's deadline, an audience's impatience, a journal's assignment, a teacher's advice—in short, because I respond to extrinsic considerations that for Derrida have no point. He hints ominously that if I violate these kinds of restraints, "the police is always waiting in the wings," precisely because the conventions that constrain interpretation "are by essence violable and precarious, *in themselves* and by the fictionality that constitutes them, even before there has been any overt transgression. . . ."[10] (My article does not get published, I flunk the course, and so forth.) Derrida contests the legitimacy, not the necessity, of boundaries.

Sometimes, to be sure, Derrida suggests not simply that we do, in practice, claim to construe the intended meaning of a text but that we should. As he notes in *Of Grammatology,*

> To produce this signifying structure [i.e., a deconstructive reading] obviously cannot consist of reproducing, by the effaced and respectful doubling of commentary, the conscious, voluntary, intentional relationship that the writer institutes in his exchanges with the history to which he belongs thanks to the element of language. This moment of doubling commentary should no doubt have its place in a critical reading. To recognize and respect all its classical exigencies is not easy and requires all the instruments of traditional criticism. Without this recognition and this respect, critical production would risk developing in any direction at all and authorize itself to say almost anything. But this indispensable guardrail has always only *protected,* it has never *opened,* a reading.[11]

By "traditional criticism," Derrida means criticism that, by effacing its own autonomy, attempts to double or reproduce what an author tries to say. Derrida here exudes respect for this kind of commentary, praising its difficulty and granting it an essential place in any critical reading, even his own, lest "critical production" scatter in "any direction at all."

This gesture of piety toward the procedures of traditional criticism conflicts with what Derrida has said elsewhere about the "fictionality that constitutes them." Even if we grant that he respects "doubling commentary," however, he is saying that while necessary, it is not sufficient. Beyond "doubling" a text, he of course advocates deconstructing it, opening interpretation to new possibilities rather than protecting its fidelity to what a text wants to say. Although assuring a certain "minimum readability" in the text, the intended meaning is nonetheless a guardrail that still permits—or fails to proscribe— limitless weaving between the lines, weavings authorized by the assumption that "the writer writes *in* a language and *in* a logic whose proper system, laws and life his discourse by definition cannot dominate absolutely."[12] And language, again, disseminates endlessly the meanings that an author tries to constrain. Even with the respect for traditional criticism that Derrida shows here, "critical production" (in theory at least) can still develop "in any direction at all and authorize itself to say almost anything."

While Derrida may account for the failures of language, he has difficulty explaining its successes. The controls of intention, context, and referent are weak when we measure them by Derrida's norms: an intention "fully present, *active* and *actual*" in the speech act it initiates; a context "absolutely determinable," "rigorous and scientific," "entirely certain"; and an omnipotent referent about which there can be no doubt. A rigid either-or, all-or-nothing logic governs Derrida's thought: because the meaning of a text is not "unique, univocal, rigorously controllable, and transmittable," it is therefore indeterminate.[13] Experience shows that the truth about interpretation lies somewhere between these two extremes. Even if we never make our meaning "absolutely determinable," we can make it clear enough to expect understanding from others, as Derrida's own practice as a writer implies.

For all his commitment to the openness of interpretation, Derrida is genuinely put out when he feels that a reader misunderstands his views.[14] In "Limited Inc abc . . . ," for instance, he accuses John Searle of misconstruing his intention. Failing to see what Derrida is "aiming at," Searle acts as if the "principal purpose" of *Sec* (the essay Searle is criticizing) consists in stating the truth. But what, Derrida asks, "if *Sec* were *doing something else*?" ("LI," 178). "How is it possible to miss the point that *Sec,* from one end to the other, is concerned with the question of truth, with the system of values associated with it . . ." ("LI," 179)? Searle also "*cuts, avoids, omits:* cutting one of the examples of *Sec* out of its dominant or most determining context; avoiding to cite more than three words; omitting the most 'important' word . . ." ("LI," 220). "By ignoring this or that moment of the text he claims to be discussing," Derrida concludes, Searle "creates for himself a version of *Sec* which is easily domesticated since it is, after all, nothing but [Searle's] own autistic representation." Derrida writes "Limited Inc . . ." "for the sake of better determining a context that [Searle] has done everything to obliterate" ("LI," 227).

These statements suggest that Derrida expects Searle to understand him. In fact, he is angrily pointing out that Searle arrives at his critique of *Sec* by misreading it—by lifting statements out of context and by assigning *Sec* an intent that Derrida rejects. Derrida's theory, it would seem, cannot explain his exasperation. Instead of rebuking Searle for misreading him, Derrida should have expected Searle to miss his point—if what *Sec* says about the "pure equivocality" of interpretation is true.

Embarrassed by Derrida's seemingly aggrieved tone in "Limited Inc. . . ," deconstructionist readers of the essay typically try to find irony in it (maybe I should say "ironize" it). Derrida, they argue, is being playful; readers who think that he is upset with Searle miss the joke. After observing, for example, that "Sarl [Derrida's name for the author(s) of Searle's critique] gravely *falsifies* matters," Derrida self-consciously pauses: "I note here that I seem to have become infected by Sarl's style: this is the first time, I believe, that I have ever accused anyone of deception, or of being deceived" ("LI," 228). Reminded of his doubts about correctness, on the next page he encloses "falsification" in quotation marks, showing that he does not take the term seriously. He does the same when he underscores the "crucial" and "important" points in *Sec* that Searle presumably has misread. The quotation marks show that these terms belong to Searle's rhetoric, not his. Derrida, then, is in this view not so much angry as amused, aware of the groundlessness of his accusations against Searle and once again belittling the game he continues to play. "What I like about this 'confrontation,'" he says, "is that I don't know if it is quite taking place, if it ever will be able, or will have been able, quite, to take place; or if it does, between whom or what" ("LI," 172).

It seems to me more accurate to say that Derrida is ambivalent, angry at Searle but not sure that he should be. His ironic disclaimers never erase the accusations that they follow; his playfulness tempers but never eliminates his anger. In any case, the ironic reading is at odds with itself, or, more exactly, with the self-mocking aim that it soberly attributes to Derrida. In appealing to the context of Derrida's writings and otherwise arguing that he means us to see that he undercuts his own complaints, this reading takes seriously the very procedures that it claims Derrida is playing with.

I say "playing with" rather than rejecting or destroying because the question that Derrida's work raises is, again, not whether we should discard the instruments of "doubling commentary," but how we should use them. Though supposedly groundless, intent, context, and so on are nevertheless powerful, language at once guaranteeing and unsettling our dependence on them. Derrida accordingly cannot lose in the exchange with Searle that I have been discussing. If, like M. H. Abrams, we object that Derrida takes seriously the rules of interpretation that underlie his rejoinder to Searle, then Derrida can reply that "Limited Inc . . ." has unwittingly demonstrated the permanent inherence of these rules in language. Abrams's charge that Derrida forbids Searle the interpretive liberties that he allows himself hits one target (Derrida's emphasis on the hollowness of the conventions that he obeys), only to miss another (his admission that we cannot avoid categories like intent and context). Derrida can claim that even as he has tried to dominate language, it has mastered him, drawing him into affirmations that language itself voids.

Conversely, if we maintain (as the ironic reading does) that after listing several apparently serious accusations against Searle, Derrida undermines them, then Derrida can argue that he is merely acknowledging their baselessness. Language has led him to subvert the protest that it encouraged him to make. Either way, whether Derrida is straightforward or self-parodying, his theory of language holds. By abdicating control over his text to language, Derrida thus becomes immune to criticism. His often noted intellectual agility or suppleness, his ability to convert attacks against his theory into compliments, paradoxically depends on his enslavement to language.

In my view, the very fact that we cannot question Derrida's theory makes it questionable, if not false. Again, he cannot be refuted because he can attribute to language whatever we say against him, arguing that we are not using language to make our point but language is using us to make its point. But because Derrida's assumptions about language cannot be denied, neither can they be tested or corrected, "testing" implying the possibility of failure and "correction" vulnerability to error. He is locked in an airtight, static view of language that he cannot verify.

Thinking that the meaning of a text must be "unique, univocal, rigorously controllable, and transmittable" to be determinate, Derrida, in short, suggests that texts (in theory) are indecipherable because language propels in multiple directions the meanings that it encourages us to try to control. Derrida nevertheless criticizes Searle for misunderstanding him, and I think that he has a right to do so—a right that our experience with language supports. We have a legitimate claim on the understanding of others, and, conversely, we have responsibilities to others (to make ourselves clear, etc.) that we can fulfill. I have been trying to show why Derrida does not persuade me to write off these claims and responsibilities as (admittedly powerful) linguistic illusions. More exactly, Derrida cannot persuade us to endorse his theory because no evidence can contradict or support it.

Other arguments for the indeterminacy of literary texts take a psychological rather than a linguistic turn but encounter difficulties similar to those that I see in Derrida. I want to mention as an especially influential example of a widespread tendency in contemporary criticism the work of Harold Bloom, whose practical criticism I will be examining in my next chapter. Bloom's well-known theory of influence does not need summarizing; I am interested here in his more general claim that in interpretation "there is always and only bias, inclination, pre-judgment, swerve" (*DC,* 9).

Despite his conviction that bias is everywhere in interpretation, Bloom is nevertheless outraged when readers find his theory "merely" his misprision, his "own paranoid code." He has deep feelings about his recent criticism but they apparently do not impinge on its validity. "I have experienced my own defensive emotions concerning the sequence of revisionary ratios that I find recurrent in so many poems, quite aside from the defensive reactions I have aroused in others. But the sequence is *there* [his emphasis] in the sense that image and trope tend to follow over-determined patterns of evasion" (*DC,* 29). Other writers do not have the option of mastering their feelings (except when they agree with Bloom); their "defensive emotions" blind them to the truth of what he says. Indeed, their anger and scorn confirm that truth by showing that Bloom has brought to light realities that they have to repress. Their denials are not disclaimers but psychologically explicable "evasions" and "idealizations"; his own conclusions are not self-serving misreadings but discoveries. The statement that "there is always and only bias" is not itself biased but absolutely true. One cannot argue for such a self-contradictory statement, and Bloom does not. He asserts it, often shrilly, appealing to his readers' reluctance to see themselves as "naïve," "sentimental," or, even worse, "idealistic" opponents of a theory in touch with the dark truths that most people try to flee. Instead of making his position more persuasive, his heated rhetoric calls attention to its illogicality.

For reasons already cited in my discussion of Derrida, the unverifiability of a critical position is a serious mark against it, not just an easily deployed quibble. Because no evidence can contradict or validate Bloom's position, he, like Derrida, is trapped in a theory that other writers can only accept, imitate, or apply. (As I will be showing in my next chapter, these other writers include poets as well as critics.) So long as he is bound to his implacable critical ideas, Bloom himself can only recycle them, contributing to the repetitiveness of his recent work. As he notes in *The Anxiety of Influence,* "a theory of poetry that presents itself as a severe poem [he means his own theory], reliant upon aphorism, apothegm, and a quite personal (though thoroughly traditional) mythic pattern, still may be judged, and may ask to be judged, as argument."[15] As argument, Bloom's defense of the necessity of misreading breaks down.

Still other arguments for indeterminacy depend on institutional rather than psychological or linguistic assumptions. The most prominent advocate of an institutional theory of interpretation is Stanley Fish, a critic who seems at first glance not to be endorsing the indeterminacy of texts but to be opposing it. Fish repeatedly declares that in practice we always expect others to understand us, just as we always declare some interpretations more correct than others. To those who fear anarchy in criticism, Fish's often quoted advice is consequently "not to worry." "No one can *be* a relativist" or thoroughgoing skeptic because

> doubting, like any other mental activity is something that one does *within* a set of assumptions that cannot at the same time be the object of doubt. . . . The project of radical doubt can never outrun the necessity of being situated; in order to doubt *everything,* including the ground one stands on, one must stand somewhere else, and that somewhere else will then be the ground on which one stands.[16]

The necessity of "being situated" is finally the necessity of choice. Dispensing with the boundaries and norms that our decisions imply is like trying to swim without water.

In emphasizing the inevitability of constraints on interpretation, Fish resembles Derrida, not, to be sure, the Derrida who is popularly imagined to think that anything goes in criticism but the more complex Derrida that I have been trying to portray in this chapter: the Derrida who places reading in concrete situations that limit it; who accepts the necessity (while questioning the legitimacy) of authorial intent, context, and other interpretive norms; and who can compare "doubling commentary" to a necessary guardrail that prevents critical production from "developing in any direction at all." In a recent article, "With the Compliments of the Author: Reflections on Austin and Derrida," Fish rightly suggests that this side of Derrida allows him to be assimilated to the theory of interpretive communities developed in Fish's *Is There a Text in This Class?*, the theory I will be examining in this chapter.[17] Admittedly there are some striking differences between Fish and Derrida. Whereas Derrida's prose is oblique and prolix, for example, Fish's style is direct and succinct. Nevertheless, overlooking Fish's theoretical affinities with Derrida makes Derrida seem too wild and Fish, I will argue, too tame.[18]

After admitting that we are not only bound but right to endorse some readings at the expense of others, Fish goes on to consider "what gives us the right so to be right" (TC, 342). As Derrida might put it, on what ground can we stand in interpretation? For Fish, we are necessarily situated in institutions or "interpretive communities" whose criteria we apply in deciding on the merits of a reading. Fish directs this answer against the "table-thumping," "Dr. Johnson-like positivist" who insists that either the facts make us right or a chaos of incommensurable interpretations results. For Fish, there are no "brute facts" in interpretation, no independent, stable text to which our readings are accountable. Interpretive strategies "dictate," "constitute," "produce," "determine," "make," "create," "generate," and "prescribe" the evidence that they call on for support. Nevertheless, because individuals share interpretive conventions, agreement can occur.

> An interpretive community is not objective because as a bundle of interests, or particular purposes and goals, its perspective is interested rather than neutral; but by the very same reasoning the meanings and texts produced by an interpretive community are not subjective because they do not proceed from an isolated individual but from a public and conventional point of view. . . . [M]embers of the same community will necessarily agree because they will see (and by seeing, make) everything in relation to that community's assumed purposes and goals; and conversely, members of different communities will disagree because from each of their respective positions the other "simply" cannot see what is obviously and inescapably there: This, then, is the explanation for the stability of interpretation among different readers (they belong to the same community). It also explains why there are disagreements and why they can be debated in a principled way: not because of a stability in the text, but because of a stability in the makeup of interpretive communities and therefore in the opposing positions they make possible. (*TC*, 14–15)

Neither arbitrary nor objective, interpretation is governed by "discourse-specific" rules.

I agree with Fish that what is noticed is what has been made noticeable by an interpretive strategy. All facts in interpretation are facts for the interpretive community that has decided to regard them as such. Failure to concede this point to Fish has stalled the argument that Ralph Rader and others have mounted against him. In "Fact, Theory, and Literary Explanation," Rader tries to locate "independently specifiable facts" in our "literary experience as it can be objectively specified, directly and indirectly." It is a fact, for example, that "we experience the speaker in Browning's 'My Last Duchess' (and cognate poems) as if he were external to us, himself visually perceivable in the setting."[19] Fish, in effect, challenges the independence of this fact by asking, Who is "we" here? Browning's speaker can be visualized only by readers who decide to read the poem this way, having mastered complex interpretive procedures that cause the speaker to appear.

These procedures themselves become visible when one interpretive community collides with another—when a Browning specialist, say, who reads the poem one way meets a class of freshmen who read it another. For the specialist to teach the freshmen, or, what is the same thing, to win them over to a professionally approved reading, it seems to me that there must be some common ground that the specialist can expand, until the unfamiliar reading extends what the students already know. If the specialist and the students occupy separate worlds, persuasion cannot occur. The students, to be sure, may still assent to the specialist's interpretation out of fear, for example, or pity. But if their decision solely results from such pressures, they have not learned anything. They have been forced to see things from a new, not necessarily better, point of view.

Like Derrida, Fish is uneasy with the distinction between force and persuasion that my example upholds.[20] For him, "the business of criticism" is not

> to determine a correct way of reading but to determine from which of a number of possible perspectives reading will proceed. This determination will not be made once and for all by a neutral mechanism of adjudication, but will be made and remade again whenever the interests and tacitly understood goals of one interpretive community replace or dislodge the interests and goals of another. The business of criticism, in other words, [is] not to decide between interpretations by subjecting them to the test of disinterested evidence but to establish by political and persuasive means (they are the same thing) the set of interpretive assumptions from the vantage of which the evidence (and the facts and the intentions and everything else) will hereafter be specifiable. (*TC*, 16)

I take "political" here to mean motivated by self-interest, not by "disinterested evidence" or the truth. In this sense of the word, complimenting the department chairman's new book may be politically shrewd, although not in accord with the facts.

If political and persuasive means are the same, then all persuasion would seem to be force and all progress simply change. Perhaps because Fish is such an engaging writer, some readers have resisted drawing this conclusion from his work. Instead of discrediting progress and knowledge, it could be argued, Fish is only redefining them. But he can say that a term like "delusion" lacks "force" and "has no operational validity" (*TC*, 390, n. 2); the same is true, by extension, of knowledge and progress. He can also contend that "intelligibility itself" is only a "fiction" (*TC*, 243). Although no longer a Bloomian wrestling match between individual readers, critical disagreement in Fish is still a power struggle among interested interpretive communities. The persistence or eminence of a critical position is due to its economic, political, and psychological appeal—to anything, in short, except its truth.

In my view, we can account for the popularity of some critical ideas this way, but not all of them. As an example of a once taboo critical position that has recently gained acceptance, Fish cites reader-response criticism, formerly discouraged by Wimsatt and Beardsley's influential article "The Affective Fallacy," but now an institutionally accepted, widely practiced methodology, the subject of forums and workshops at every MLA convention and the concern of numerous books and articles sanctioned by major university presses. The elevation of reader-response criticism from a fallacy to a methodology has brought to light "a whole new set of facts to which its practitioners can now refer," including "patterns of expectation," "textual gaps," and "reversals of direction," to name only a few (*TC*, 344–45). "Of course," Fish concludes, quoting Wayne Booth, we are still "'right to rule out at least some readings,' but there is now one less reading or kind of reading that can be ruled out, because there is now one more interpretive procedure that has been accorded a place in the literary institution" (*TC*, 345).

While everything that Fish says about the reception of reader-response criticism seems to me true, it does not follow that this kind of criticism owes its ascendancy to "politics" rather than to a better understanding of literature. Some critics may have embraced affective criticism because it allowed them to write an article, please a colleague, or vent their long-standing personal hatred of Wimsatt and Beardsley. But such motives cannot explain the widespread interest in reader-response criticism of so many critics, some of them former adherents of the New Criticism. As Fish admits, "quite often we find it inconvenient to believe the things we currently believe, but we find too that it is impossible not to believe them" (*TC*, 362). The intellectual necessity that inheres in some beliefs explains their broad appeal, preventing their reduction to bias, if not establishing them as true for all time.

Like his account of reader-response criticism, Fish's view of his own development as a critic casts doubt on his theory. When he looks over his career in *Is There a Text in This Class?*, he sees progress, certain truths "becoming clearer and clearer" (*TC*, 68). It was a "large mistake," for example, to think that *Coriolanus* is a play about speech acts, as he did in "How To Do Things with Austin and Searle" (*TC*, 200). Similarly, because he has changed his mind about pastoral, he no longer sees what once seemed "obvious and indisputable" in Spenser's "Shepheardes Calendar," even though he consequently has had to discard "some of the set-pieces with which [he] used to adorn [his] teaching" (*TC*, 364). Fish tries to discount his sense of progress, but I do not see why he should. In his view,

> a revolution in one's beliefs will always feel like a progress, even though, from the outside, it will have the appearance merely of a change. . . . We can't help thinking that our present views are sounder than those we used to have or those professed by others. . . . In other words, the idea of progress is inevitable, not, however, because there *is* progress in the sense of a clearer and clearer sight of an independent object but because the *feeling* of having progressed is an inevitable consequence of the firmness with which we hold our beliefs, or, to be more precise, of the firmness with which our beliefs hold us. (*TC*, 361–62)

The fact that "a revolution in one's beliefs will always feel like a progress" does not mean that progress has not occurred. The feeling that we have learned something, in other words, may be inevitable, self-congratulatory, gratifying, *and* true. Progress can be seen from some "outside" perspective as change—and still be progress.

Fish has not shown that progress cannot take place, but I have not shown that it can. Another one of his examples suggests to me that we have learned something about literature. To illustrate a discredited but potentially plausible interpretive judgment, Fish proposes to read Blake's "The Tyger" as "an allegory of the digestive processes,"

> a first-person lament of someone who had violated a dietary prohibition against eating tiger meat, and finds that forbidden food burning brightly in his stomach, making its fiery way through the forests of the intestinal tract, beating and hammering like some devil-wielded anvil. In his distress he can do nothing but rail at the tiger and the mischance that led him to mistake its meat for the meat of some purified animal: "Did he who made the Lamb make thee?" The poem ends as it began, with the speaker still paying the price of his sin and wondering at the inscrutable purpose of a deity that would lead his creatures into digestive temptation. (*TC*, 348–49)

Fish pounces on the reply that he hopes to provoke, namely, that the facts prove his reading wrong. Interpretations, again, constitute the facts that they ostensibly depend on for confirmation. Because "canons of acceptability" change, moreover, what is ridiculous today may be "respectable and even orthodox" tomorrow. In the case of Blake, virtually anything goes, "because according to the critical consensus there is no belief so bizarre that Blake could not have been committed to it and it would be no trick at all to find some elaborate system of alimentary significances (Pythagorean? Swedenborgian? Cabbalistic?) which he could be presumed to have known" (*TC*, 348). Fish challenges any reader who thinks he has gone too far "to consult some recent numbers of *Blake Studies*" (*TC*, 349).

As Fish realizes, to gain a hearing his reading has to build on the critical consensus it wants to extend or subvert (just as in my earlier example the specialist and the students have to find some common ground). He cannot impose on Blake any "elaborate system of alimentary significances"; because of what critics already presume to know about Blake, only something like a Swedenborgian system will do. When we examine our presumptions about Blake, however, we find that some have endured longer or have won the assent of a broader range of critics than others. Fish does not want to say that the persistence of these assumptions is in their favor—that they have lasted, in other words, because they work as interpretations of Blake. But he is at a loss to improve on the cognitive explanation he wants to discard. Inertia, prejudice, and institutional fiat will not explain the durability of these interpretations (even if prejudice were the answer, we would still need to know why these "prejudices" about Blake have survived while so many others have disappeared or have excited vigorous opposition). I would suggest that some presumptions about Blake endure because they satisfy our sense of what he says: they are more clearly right than others. The fact that everyone (including, of course, Stanley Fish) rejects a gastrointestinal approach to "The Tyger," that no one has found an appropriate system of dietary restrictions to which Blake could be thought to have subscribed, makes Fish's reading unlikely, if not, to be sure, impossible.

As Fish says, "no reading, however outlandish it might appear, is inherently an impossible one" (*TC*, 347). But it does not follow that we cannot have a fairly good idea of what a text says. For Fish, because "What is noticed has been *made* noticeable . . . by an interpretive strategy," we cannot claim that what we notice is there, prior to our noticing it. To cite one last example, in demonstrating that "our notions of the 'same' or 'different' texts are fictions," Fish observes that he reads two presumably different texts, "Lycidas" and "The Waste Land," in the same way. Therefore, "the answer to the question 'why do different texts give rise to different sequences of interpretive acts?' is that *they don't have to,* an answer which implies strongly that 'they' don't exist" (*TC*, 170). But the fact that we can read "The Waste Land" and "Lycidas" the same way may mean that in this way the texts are similar, not that they do not exist. Fish's example again fails to justify his skepticism.

Fish, to be sure, is not alone in inferring that an entity is not there because an interpretive convention has produced it. Self-described Wittgensteinian or institutional approaches to interpretation often make this leap. To show that we define concepts by their use, John Ellis (in *The Theory of Literary Criticism*) uses the example of weeds: "weeds are plants that we do not wish to cultivate," a definition that is admittedly circular (weeds are what we weed) and evaluative (we eradicate them because in some circumstances we do not value them). Because no physical properties set off weeds (they come in all sizes, not all of them are especially hardy, and so forth), weeds are what we agree to call weeds. It is accordingly "not difficult to see that there is a certain sense in which weeds do not exist until we make them into weeds" (for example, weeds do not exist for the child who has not been taught what they are, as any parent with a garden can testify). All of this seems to me true. But it still does not follow that weeds and other such categories "organize the world rather than describe it," the

conclusion Ellis draws from this example.[21] Such conventional categories may describe the world as well as organize it. The fact that we
create the term, that a weed in one setting may be a flower in another,
does not mean that the referent of the term is not there.

To return to Fish: much as Derrida's theory invokes an unrealistic
choice between all or nothing, Fish's association of knowledge with
certainty fractures his position into a series of non sequiturs. Because
we cannot determine the validity of a reading "once and for all by a
neutral mechanism of adjudication," we are left with a pointless succession of "community-specific" decisions.[22] But some of these decisions, in my view, deserve more respect than others. The community
that calls *Macbeth* a tragedy includes virtually everyone; this judgment
about the play is therefore probably correct. As John Reichert points
out, "Who among us . . . whatever the object of interpretation, would
choose one hypothesis over another on the grounds of its greater
inconsistency, or on the grounds of its accounting for fewer of the
facts that we want to explain, or on the grounds of its being unnecessarily complicated?"[23] "Us" here implies an interpretive community
but one that is broad enough to suggest that consistency, thor-
oughness, and efficiency are valid norms.

I am not arguing that the majority is always right, only that it can be
right. And when an interpretive community embraces multitudes,
like the community that terms *Macbeth* a tragedy, it probably is right. I
know no better way of accounting for a consensus that includes
Samuel Johnson, Karl Marx, and John Keats.

The recent work of J. Hillis Miller, a widely read Yale deconstructionist, brings together many of the ideas I have been criticizing in this
chapter. In his early work on deconstruction, Miller dispenses with
truth in interpretation, only to hold texts accountable to an invidious
norm. In "Deconstructing the Deconstructers," his review of Joseph
Riddel's *The Inverted Bell*, he accuses Riddel of distorting Heidegger
and Derrida. After making this objection, he softens it. Admittedly, he
concedes, Heidegger and Derrida are difficult writers to get right.
Their prose is hard even for native German and French speakers,
both draw on difficult precursors, and English translations of each
writer are often misleading, when they are available at all. After making this concession, Miller eliminates the objection that prompted it.
What does it mean, he asks himself, to be "true" to Heidegger and

Derrida? Who is this "Derrida," this "Heidegger"? Mastering other languages, reading more of each writer, exploring their precursors—these activities only defer the normative reading that they promise. "The apparently solid basis for interpretation"—for criticizing a book like Riddel's—"becomes a labyrinth of endless wanderings, including wanderings back to the precursors of the precursors, the labyrinths behind, within, or beneath each labyrinth."

Although Miller dissolves his original objection, he never quite gives it up. Riddel's book, he concludes, is self-contradictory, inconsistent, and heterogeneous; it speaks in terms of origins after denying them. But, recalling a move of Derrida's that I discussed earlier, Miller goes on to conclude that language explains this wavering, not corrigible error. Texts are necessarily heterogeneous because they are texts; no author can escape Riddel's blindness.

> Riddel's book may in fact have its greatest value in its apparently unintentional demonstration of the irreducible heterogeneity of the languages of poetry, of philosophy, and of criticism. A corollary of this would be the fact that deconstructive criticism can never reach a clarity which is not vulnerable to being deconstructed in its turn. However clarified, refined, or sophisticated Riddel were to become it would still be possible to show that his work is incoherent.

Riddel at least tries to avoid reference, or, more precisely, to undercut the references he cannot help making. In Miller's view, Hugh Kenner, who treats poems as manmade objects in *A Homemade World*, does not even question the boundaries, origins, and ends of the poems he discusses. William Carlos Williams's poetry (Miller's focus here) "opens itself to Kenner's reading as well as to Riddel's," just as Kenner's reading itself presumably has its self-deconstructive, Derridean side. What puts Riddel closer than Kenner to "what is at stake in Williams' work" is his greater awareness that Williams "puts all origin in question and gives to language a generative power, even a power to generate . . . nostalgia for the absent origin."[24] Kenner, in short, glosses over the generative power of language. Riddel recognizes it, yet occasionally forgets it. So, apparently, does Williams.

Miller here rejects truth to a particular text as his criterion, only to install in its place truth to textuality as Derrida and others have defined it. Applying this norm, distinguishing "more or less self-aware" uses of language, depends on insight into the intention of an author, which the norm itself discourages. If texts are the effects of language, then why should we even care to know what the author is trying to do? If, more importantly, the self is a "linguistic construction," an "effect of language," rather than "a solid *point de depart*," then Miller's normative distinctions between Kenner and Riddel rest on a fiction.[25] An author does not give language generative power; language displays its power over a text with or without the author's permission, if indeed we can even speak of an "author" here.

I am not exaggerating the authority Miller invests in language. In "The Critic as Host," for instance, he hardens the generative power of language into an "inexorable law" (*DC*, 226), which all texts "necessarily" (with or without their author's consent) obey. In Miller's view, everything is "undecidable" except his own assumption that all texts are undecidable because, again, they forever undo the propositions that they make. Deconstruction, which respects this ceaseless double movement, is accordingly not merely one more kind of criticism but "interpretation as such":

> "Deconstruction" is neither nihilism nor metaphysics but simply interpretation as such, the untangling of the inherence of metaphysics in nihilism and of nihilism in metaphysics by way of the close reading of texts. This procedure, however, can in no way escape, in its own discourse, from the language of the passages it cites. This language is the expression of the inherence of nihilism in metaphysics and of metaphysics in nihilism. We have no other language. The language of criticism is subject to exactly the same limitations and blind alleys as the language of the works it reads. The most heroic effort to escape from the prisonhouse of language only builds the walls higher. (*DC*, 230)

One wonders how Miller gets outside the prison house of language to see its walls. He does not; indeed, he cannot, for "there is no escape" (*DC*, 231). Instead of proving that language traps us, he caricatures efforts to use words as instruments of discovery or communication. The critic, for instance, experiences his enclosure in the language of the text he interprets "as his failure to get his poet right in a final decisive formulation which will allow him to have done with that poet, once and for all" (*DC*, 247–48). As in Derrida, a starkeither-or logic is at work here. Either we get a poet right in one "final decisive formulation" or we find ourselves lost with our author in the "blind alleys" of language. Either we can seize the meaning of texts in "a single, definitive interpretation" or they are "unreadable" (*DC*, 226).[26] Miller never pauses to consider that possibilities may exist between these extremes: that criticism may illuminate a text without exhausting discussion of it, and that not even the most ardent partisan of objectivity in criticism expects to interpret a work and be finished with it. By trivializing opposing views, he keeps his own invulnerable.

An ironclad, unverifiable assumption about writing like Miller's necessarily overpowers everything in its path. No textual evidence can challenge his theory of language because texts become texts by complying with it. Miller and the critics he has influenced are accordingly not content to explain some texts; they have the keys to all texts. In recent deconstructive criticism, writers as different as Hawthorne, Dickens, Balzac, George Eliot, Sidney, Goethe, Wordsworth, Williams, Conrad, and even Homer end up displaying much the same "self-subverting heterogeneity."[27] What happens within texts also takes place between them. In "Critic as Host" and other essays Miller uses supplementarity, the endless making and unmaking of assertion, to chart: (1) literary genres ("it is characteristic of realistic fiction as a genre," for example, both to assert and to undermine the dependency of selfhood "on intersubjective lines");[28] (2) the relation of a text to its precursors (putting Bloom's theory in grammatological terms, Miller notes that each work tries to appear self-begotten by "erasing" its predecessors who nevertheless survive as "traces" in the still incomplete work that results); (3) the relation of texts within an author's canon ("The same scene, with the same elements in a slightly different arrangement, is written by Shelley over and over again from *Queen Mab* to *The Triumph of Life,* in a repetition ended only with his death. This repetition mimes the poet's failure ever to get it right and so end the necessity of trying once more with what remains" [*DC,* 237]); (4) the relation of one reading to another (each critic attempts to see further than the other, only to end up together in the maze of language, the very maze that prompted the search for clarity); (5) the relation of a reading to a literary work (rather than "surveying the text with sovereign command from outside," criticism "remains caught within the activity in the text it retraces" [*DC,* 251]); and (6) the relation of a literary work to "experience," "real life" being "only another way of dwelling within signs after all" (*DC,* 246).

Because his all-encompassing commitment to textuality dictates his response to particular texts, Miller's criticism, like Bloom's, has thus become monotonous, predictably finding reinforcement for Derrida's theory of writing wherever Miller looks. As if aware of this objection to his work, in his latest book, *Fiction and Repetition,* Miller has begun speaking of his readings as hypotheses, to be supported or refuted by additional evidence, not simply accepted on the say-so of Derrida. The evidence, however, is still not in his favor.

An especially clear illustration of Miller's deconstructive strategy, *Fiction and Repetition* discovers repetition not only in the recurrence of images, statements, and incidents within a text but also in the relationship between a text and what lies outside it: the conventions and precursors that the text recapitulates, the personal experience that it reviews, even the critical readings it inspires. Asking a by now familiar question, Miller wants to know "what controls the meaning these repetitions create?"[29] Do texts have determinate meanings that critics can discover, or are texts undecidable, open to a variety of readings? Deploring the separation between theoretical and practical criticism—a point to which I will return in my next chapter—Miller examines these questions as they arise in several nineteenth- and twentieth-century English novels, including such often discussed texts as *Lord Jim, Tess of the D'Urbervilles, Wuthering Heights,* and *Mrs. Dalloway.*

Miller's study of these novels characteristically rests on the assumption, stated in his first chapter, that there are only two ways of understanding repetition. A "Platonic" theory appeals to "a solid archetypal model which is untouched by the effects of repetition" (*FR,* 6). In this view, an ideal bed centers or grounds the particular beds that "repeat" it, just as, by extension, a fixed referent guarantees the truth of texts that imitate it. A "Nietzschean mode of repetition," by contrast, "posits a world based on difference" (*FR,* 6). Instead of deriving from—in Miller's terms, "repeating"—an external *point de départ,* particulars differ from each other in a chain that has no beginning, center, or end. Miller's thesis is that each of the novels he studies demonstrates the "necessary inherence, one in the other" of these two polarized forms of repetition, showing that "each form of repetition inevitably calls up the other as its shadow companion. You cannot have one without the other, though each subverts the other" (*FR,* 16). By "intertwining" these two incompatible forms of repetition, Miller's examples accordingly defy the law of noncontradiction: "the repetitive series is presented as both grounded and ungrounded at once" (*FR,* 17). The "alogic" of these texts accounts for their "heterogeneity," their ineradicable "strangeness" and "oddness," and their capacity to authorize logically incongruous readings among which the critic can never decide.

Although obviously indebted to deconstruction, Miller's analyses avoid the shortcomings that many critics, myself included, have found in deconstructionist writing. His book exemplifies clarity, generosity toward other critics (even those who have sharply criticized him), unpretentious erudition, attention to detail, and caution. Nevertheless, despite Miller's care, his larger conclusions still seem to me unpersuasive, for reasons that become clear when his argument is broken down into what I see as its four steps: (1) Appearing to affirm the "Platonic" form of repetition, the texts discussed by Miller presumably invite the reader to look for "a single explanatory principle or cause," "possessed of full explanatory power over the whole network of signs which it has generated and which it controls, giving each sign its deferred meaning" (FR, 60). (2) Claiming to be the "Daniel who can at last decipher the writing on the wall," critics, with "confident certainty," have presented what they think is "the definitive rational explanation of the text in question" (FR, 49–50)—the "single explanatory principle" that the text encourages them to seek. (3) In a "Nietzschean" act of demystification, however, the text unravels the patterns that it inspires its readers to construct, leaving "no visible thematic or structural principle which will allow the reader to find its secret, explicate it once and for all, untie all its knots and straighten all its threads" (FR, 25). (4) Instead of unambiguously settling on a "fixed pattern of meaning," the text, then, "oscillates" or "vibrates" among multiple "possibilities of meaning." Because these possibilities are "rigorously delimited by the text," the text is not indeterminate "in the sense of being indefinitely multiple and nebulous." Rather, its indeterminacy "lies in the multiplicity of possible incompatible explanations given by the novel and in the lack of evidence justifying a choice of one over the others. The reader cannot logically have them all, and yet nothing he is given determines a choice among them. . . . Each calls up the others, but it does not make sense to have more than one of them" (FR, 40).

Although I have misgivings about the first two steps in this argument, I am most uneasy with the move from step three to four. If Miller were only contesting the claim of a critic to explain the whole text—to offer the final (or only) word on the subject, leaving nothing for anyone else to say—then his argument would be a valuable illustration of the principle, defended by Wayne C. Booth and others, that because texts are "over-rich" or "overdetermined," monistic explanations distort them. But Miller seems to be saying that critics are wrong not simply in thinking that they have explained all of the text but in thinking they have explained the text at all. He speaks of the critic failing to "ever lucidly understand the text" or "ever have rational mastery over it" (*FR*, 63). In Miller's view, a pattern assigned to the text is not simply one among many; it is not there. More exactly, we attribute a shape to the text only by ignoring the gaps, smudges, and inconsistencies that undermine our attribution. Revising an interpretative guess in one place only causes trouble in another. It follows that instead of complementing one another—in Miller's words, instead of building "on one another according to some ideal of progressive elucidation" (*FR*, 50)—our suppositions about the text cancel each other out. Although each reading "calls up" what we hope will be a more adequate one, the effort to end the series of unsatisfying interpretations only prolongs it. We are left with "an interplay among a definable and limited set of possibilities, all of which have force, but all of which may not logically have force at once" (*FR*, 127).

I agree that different interpretations which aim at totally elucidating the same text are incompatible. It is a contradiction to say that Tess (in *Tess of the d'Urbervilles*) is simply the victim of changes in nineteenth-century England and merely the slave of her passions (to borrow one of Miller's examples). But I cannot imagine a competent reader saying either one of these things about Tess, let alone both. (Not wishing to "disrupt unnecessarily" his discussion with "manifold indications of indebtedness, agreement, or disagreement," Miller tends to summarize in general terms the critical studies that he cites, leaving me with the impression that he exaggerates the confidence of the readers he criticizes.) Readers more commonly assert that history and personality—along with gender, place of birth, and many other things, if not everything—contribute to Tess's development. These critics, I would argue, are responding to the novel, which urges us to discover multiple causes for Tess's actions, not just one.

It is true that Hardy rejects facile explanations for what happens to Tess, especially optimistic explanations that would offer some rationale or cure for her suffering. The following passage, quoted by Miller, typifies Hardy's severity:

> We may wonder whether at the acme and summit of the human progress these anachronisms will be corrected by a finer intuition, a closer

interaction of the social machinery than that which now jolts us round
and along; but such completeness is not to be prophesied, or even
conceived possible. Enough that in the present case, as in millions, it
was not the two halves of a perfect whole that confronted each other at
the perfect moment; a missing counterpart wandered independently
about the earth waiting in crass obtuseness till the late time came. Out
of which maladroit delay sprang anxieties, disappointments, shocks,
catastrophes, and passing-strange destinies.

Even if nineteenth-century England were a better world in the novel,
or Tess a better person, the "mismatching of man and woman" (*FR*,
134) could still occur. But while progress would not magically eliminate Tess's pain, an irrational society has nevertheless added to it.
Instead of concluding with Miller that "the design [of *Tess*] has no
source" (*FR*, 141), I would accordingly say that it has several, which,
taken together, help us to understand her predicament, if not solve it.

Each step of Miller's argument, in short, seems to me shaky. I cannot think of many nineteenth- and twentieth-century novels that
promise their readers definitive mastery of all their secrets, or many
readers who hope to explicate texts and be done with them. And
although a "single explanatory principle" may not tie up all the loose
ends of a text, several explanations may shed light on its "pattern of
meaning," if not explain it once and for all. Surprisingly, given his
Derridean skepticism toward assertions of presence, Miller (unlike
Fish) speaks of the text as an independent object or force, rigorously
constraining our attempts to make sense of it. In the view of interpretation that I have been endorsing in this chapter, the presence that
Miller grants the text also applies to many (though not all) of the
patterns discerned in it, allowing interpretations to cohere and progress rather than clash and go nowhere.

Elsewhere I hope to further support this view; here, however, I
have been trying to explain why Derrida, Bloom, Fish, and Miller do
not persuade me to relinquish it. Each of these critics seems to me to
reject one untenable theory of meaning, only to embrace another.
They rightly argue that we cannot be "entirely certain" about the
meaning of a literary work, that the context of a text is never "absolutely determinable," that interpretative decisions cannot "be made
once and for all by a neutral mechanism of adjudication," and that no
"single explanatory principle" can illuminate a text "once and for all,
untie all its knots and straighten all its threads." But it follows for

these critics that context, intent, evidence, and other limits on interpretation are therefore linguistic illusions (Derrida), fraudulent conventions that conceal self-defensive warfare among individual readers
(Bloom), hollow norms at the mercy of the authorities that have the
power to define them (Fish), and crude attempts to stabilize texts that
will not stand still (Miller). Even as these critics thus debunk constraints on interpretation, they nevertheless invoke them when they
claim, for example, to offer an accurate description of literary history
(in the case of Bloom) or when they think that a reader has miscon-
strued their own work, neglected its "dominant or most determining
context," and otherwise missed what they are "aiming at" (to quote
Derrida's rejoinder to Searle). Each of these critics is then in the
awkward position of trying to explain (or explain away) his confidence
in his own readings and his insistence on controls that presumably
have no cognitive point. I have been suggesting that these explanations fail, leaving these critics at a loss to improve on the cognitive
account of interpretation that they wish to question. My point is not
that Derrida, say, is right when he complains that Searle misreads him
but that such an interpretative judgment can be right, though not
"entirely certain."

IV

Revisionist Criticism in Practice

Advocates of "revisionist criticism," to use Geoffrey Hartman's phrase, increasingly defend it not on the theoretical grounds that I examine in my preceding chapter but as "close," "rigorous," or "slow" reading. Harold Bloom, for instance, repeatedly asserts that he is trying to enrich practical criticism by devising stronger, more imaginative readings of particular texts. Echoing Paul de Man, J. Hillis Miller similarly challenges critics of deconstruction to assess it by its interpretive results:

> In recent controversies about criticism there has been, so it seems to me, too much attention paid to this theory or that, to its terminology, and to its presumed or "theoretical" consequences, and not enough to the readings made possible by the theories in question. A theory is all too easy to refute or deny, but a reading can be controverted only by going through the difficult task of rereading the work in question and proposing an alternative reading. (*FR*, 21)

Taking up Miller's challenge, I continue my critique of revisionist criticism by studying how three poststructuralist critics—Bloom, Paul de Man, and Tilottama Rajan—read a specific poem, Shelley's *The Triumph of Life*.

My aim here is to assess the rigor of these three readings (or readers), but the fact that my example is a romantic poem touches on still another claim made on behalf of recent theory, namely, that it especially deepens our understanding of romantic literature. In Hartman's words, "the revaluation of Romanticism is a special feature of post–New Critical or revisionist criticism in America": "if there is one criterion that distinguishes the present movement in criticism from that prevailing, more or less, since Eliot, it is a better understanding and higher evaluation of the Romantic and nineteenth-century writers" (*CW,* 44, 46). In addition to questioning the interpretative gains permitted by a commitment to textual indeterminacy, I will also be arguing that Hartman's claim is unfounded, at least in this particular case.

In keeping with a basic scholarly convention, Bloom, Rajan, and de Man, despite their other differences, open their readings of *The Triumph of Life* by citing other commentators on Shelley, all of them well-known romanticists: M. H. Abrams, Northrop Frye, Donald Reiman, Carlos Baker, Kenneth Neill Cameron, and the Harold Bloom of *Shelley's Mythmaking* (Bloom's first book). In revisionist terms, these critics are idealistic or naïve (they read *The Triumph* as a straightforward expression of its author's conscious intentions); logocentric (they find a determinate reference, or range of references, in the text); and optimistic (they shelter Shelley's affirmations from his doubts and second thoughts). The interpretations of these critics, moreover, have acquired "canonical" status, familiarity with their readings being one way academic critics measure competence in romantic literature.

Rajan's references to Abrams and to Earl Wasserman are typical. While Wasserman "discusses Shelley's skepticism at length, he seems to regard it as intermediate rather than terminal."[1] He does not even deal with *The Triumph of Life* in *Shelley: A Critical Reading.* Similarly, although Abrams acknowledges a "darker side of Romanticism" (19), he, too, makes the romantics' doubts "intermediate rather than terminal" (18). In his reading of *The Triumph,* Life, a grotesque figure in a chariot who triumphantly leads a procession of his captives, stands for "the material and sensual conditions of everyday existence which solicit, depress, and corrupt the aspiring human spirit," conditions which overcome all but a "sacred few."[2] Shelley narrates the "bleak facts" of his poem, however, with "the verve of a poet who has tapped new sources of creative strength," and he sets his dream vision "in the frame of a joyous morning in spring," perhaps suggesting that he counts himself among the "sacred few" and that he contemplates escaping or reversing the defeat of human potentiality that he finds in history.[3] Because the poem is unfinished, Abrams admittedly speculates about its resolution.

Rajan astutely connects Abrams's optimistic reading to an organic

theory of poetry which makes the text "a complex harmony: an organic structure whose unity is strengthened rather than undermined
by the presence of irony, ambiguity, and paradox. Such a view of
poetry, because it makes the poet into the great reconciler, sustains
rather than questions the constructive authority of imagination" (18).
Such a view, Rajan might have added, also matches some of Shelley's
own ideas about poetry, at least as he expressed them in *A Defence of
Poetry* and in his Prefaces to *The Revolt of Islam* and *Prometheus Unbound.* Abrams rebukes those scholars who do not take Shelley's constructive intentions seriously, who look back "at earlier literature
through the gloomy contemporary perspective" and conclude that
"Romantic writers could not really have meant what they claimed,
hence that they must have been self-divided, or even unconsciously
committed to the negations of the positives they so confidently asserted." If the romantics' "affirmations strike a contemporary ear as
deluded or outworn, that may be the index of their relevance to an
age of profounder dereliction and dismay than Shelley and
Wordsworth knew."[4]

After citing these "canonical" interpretations, Rajan, de Man, and
Bloom proceed in different ways to dispute them. Bloom focuses on
the chariot in the poem and suggests that the chariot has always been
an image of "transumption"; writers from Ezekiel to Milton have used
the image to mask or redeem their belatedness by suggesting that
earlier uses of the image merely figure forth its appearance in their
work. In *The Triumph of Life* Shelley, in Bloom's view, uses this image
against Wordsworth, whose influence he is trying to vanquish. Rousseau, who at first glance looks like an "old root" growing out of the
hillside, is Wordsworth's surrogate in the poem. The "Shape all light"
that induces Rousseau to join the procession of victims represents
Wordsworthian nature (hence the allusions to the "Immortality" ode
that surround Rousseau's encounter with the Shape). Natural piety,
instead of freeing Rousseau (i.e., Wordsworth), plunges him into the
procession that follows the chariot. Bloom seems to agree with Abrams on the significance of Life, the Charioteer; in fact, he says,
"there is no mystery about Life in *The Triumph of Life*": "Life is precisely what has triumphed over Wordsworth and Coleridge, that is,
over their imaginative integrity and autonomy as strong poets."[5] Shelley, in short, wins his freedom from these two precursors by linking
their faith in nature to their subsequent decline into religious or-

thodoxy and political conservatism, a decline that he represents by Rousseau's capitulation to the chariot of Life.

But Wordsworth is "a dangerous opponent to take on," and Shelley's victory over him is "equivocal" (98). Limiting Wordsworth's influence entails a costly self-curtailment, "a powerful repression of Shelley's own desire to carry through the Rousseau-Wordsworth dream of natural redemption" (100). What Shelley gains from Wordsworth he accordingly "loses to time or to language, both of which become more problematic in the *Triumph* than they are in Wordsworth" (98). Bloom does not illustrate this point, but he implies that when Shelley renounces nature, he also seems to give up on life, death being the only way left of escaping the degradations of everyday existence. His last poem is "sublimely suicidal."

The fact that Shelley's (accidental) death prevented him from finishing the poem seems to mean less to Bloom than to Abrams, because in Bloom's view

> . . . there are, of course, no "unfinished" strong poems; there are only stronger and weaker poems. The idea of a "finished" poem itself depends upon the absurd, hidden notion that reifies poems from relationships into entities. As a poem is not even so much a relationship between entities, as it is a relationship between relationships, or a Peircean Idea of Thirdness, we can say that no relationship between relationships can ever be finished *or* unfinished except quite arbitrarily. (99)

The Wordsworth whom Shelley battles in *The Triumph* is himself the (unfinished) product of a comparable struggle not only with Milton but with later poets who have tried to make us read him differently. Seeing poems as open-ended relationships in this way obviously blurs their boundaries. *The Triumph* is no more finished (or unfinished) than any other poem.

Paul de Man notes at the outset of "Shelley Disfigured" that *The Triumph* is a fragment upon which much "archeological labor" has been expended (*DC,* 39). From the pieces of the poem that Shelley has left us, critics have tried to infer the shape of the whole. We have, moreover, questioned the poem with "an edge of urgency" (*DC,* 40), because it dates from the period in which we tend to locate the origins or antecedents of our own politics, thought, and literature. What does it mean, de Man asks, to assign a shape to a poem and, more generally, to see romanticism itself as a moment in a larger process that includes us? What right do we have to call a text or a historical period a fragment that we can reconstruct and complete?

De Man correctly notes that the questions critics have asked *of* the poem repeat the questions asked *in* the poem when the narrator (de Man calls him Shelley) confronts Rousseau. Optimistic critics (like Donald Reiman) have argued that Shelley learns from the questions he asks Rousseau; Rousseau's capitulation serves as a warning that Shelley heeds. Instead of seeing intellectual growth in the poem, de Man finds an infinite regress of questions that frustrates rather than enlightens Rousseau, Shelley, and, by extension, the reader. In a "key passage," for example, Rousseau encounters the "Shape all light" and says, "Shew whence I came, and where I am, and why" (l. 398). "Arise and quench thy thirst," she replies (l. 400). Instead of drinking knowledge from the cup that she offers him, Rousseau is further confused. Shelley has him say (in lines de Man quotes),

> "I rose; and bending at her sweet command,
> Touched with faint lips the cup she raised,
> And suddenly my brain became as sand
>
> "Where the first wave had more than half erased
> The track of deer on desert Labrador,
> Whilst the fierce wolf from which they fled amazed
>
> "Leaves his stamp visibly upon the shore
> Until the second bursts—so on my sight
> Burst a new Vision never seen before.—"
>
> (ll. 402–10)

According to de Man, this scene dramatizes "the failure to satisfy a desire for self-knowledge," a failure that the poem repeats in a "movement of effacing and of forgetting" that "dispels any illusion of dialectical progress or regress" (*DC*, 45, 44). In this passage, Rousseau's metamorphosis (not to be glossed over as his growth) is "said to be the erasure of an imprinted track, a passive, mechanical operation that is no longer within the brain's own control: both the production and the erasure of the track are not an act performed by the brain, but the brain being acted upon by something else" (*DC*, 45–46).

This "something else" turns out to be language. More specifically, the "Shape all light" stands for the "figurality of all signification" (*DC*, 62). In the poem, questions give way to other questions; figures erase other figures, as the stamp of the wolf displaces the track of the deer; and knowledge collapses into an indeterminate state in which we think we have forgotten something but cannot be sure. All of this happens because the poem dramatizes the power of language to undermine the assertions that language encourages in an endless process that "glimmers, hovers, and wavers, but refuses to yield the clarity it keeps announcing" (*DC*, 53). Language, as emblematized in the "Shape all light," accounts for the poem's oscillating imagery and repetitive, open-ended structure.

In a tortuous but, I think, representative exhibition of deconstructionist close reading, de Man presumes to pinpoint the entrance of language into the poem. As Rousseau watches the Shape, he at first sees her softly treading the waves and gliding along the air, then feels her feet "blot / The thoughts of him who gazed on them," until soon

> "All that was, seemed as if it had been not;
> And all the gazer's mind was strewn beneath
> Her feet like embers; and she, thought by thought,
>
> Trampled its fires into the dust of death. . . ."

                                                                (ll. 385–88)

A shift in sound accompanies what de Man sees as the "increased violence" of the Shape: the Shape glides in harmony with the melodious sounds of nature and the water, then moves (Shelley says) "in a measure new" when she tramples the mind of her observer. "Measure" is the key here. By distilling measure from melody and harmony, the poem acknowledges the mastery of language.

> Measure is articulated sound, that is to say language. Language rather than music, in the traditional sense of harmony and melody. . . . The "tread" of this dancer, which needs a ground to the extent that it carries the weight of gravity, is no longer melodious, but reduces music to the mere measure of repeated articulations. It singles out from music the accentual or tonal punctuation which is also present in spoken diction. . . . The thematization of language in *The Triumph of Life* occurs at this point, when "measure" separates from the phenomenal aspects of signification as a *representation*, and stresses instead the literal and material aspects of language. . . . It is tempting to interpret this event, the shape's "trampling" the fires of thought "into the dust of

death" (1. 388), certainly the most enigmatic moment in the poem, as
the bifurcation between the semantic and the non-signifying, material
properties of language. (*DC*, 59–60)

After this event Rousseau drinks from the cup and succumbs to the
procession. Significantly, de Man adds, the rainbow that first appeared with the Shape reappears "as a rigid, stony arch said 'fiercely
[to extoll] the fortune' of the shape's defeat by what the poem calls
'life' " (*DC*, 58). The first rainbow is a figure for the "unity of percep-
tion and cognition undisturbed by the possibly disruptive mediation
of its own figuration" (*DC*, 58). The defeat of this rainbow confirms
that language, momentarily forgotten, has rigidly reasserted itself,
proclaiming the merely figurative status of what we thought was
knowledge and spurring the futile search for literal or objective truth.

The Triumph of Life, in short, announces the triumph of language:
over Rousseau (when he drinks the cup and joins the procession),
over Shelley (when his effort to learn the truth from Rousseau dissolves into an endless series of questions and metaphors), and over
the reader (when our interrogation of the text and of romanticism
reaches a similar impasse). In de Man, as in Bloom, the fragmentary
status of this text turns out to challenge the wholeness of all texts. All
texts, as well as all historical periods, are arbitrarily broken-off fragments to which we attribute a spurious coherence and wholeness:

> It may seem a freak of chance to have a text thus molded by an actual
> occurrence [Shelley's drowning], yet the reading of *The Triumph of Life*
> establishes that this mutilated textual model exposes the wound of a
> fracture that lies hidden in all texts. If anything, this text is more rather
> than less typical than texts that have not thus been truncated. . . . *The
> Triumph of Life* warns us that nothing, whether deed, word, thought or
> text, ever happens in relation, positive or negative, to anything that
> precedes, follows or exists elsewhere, but only as a random event
> whose power, like the power of death, is due to the randomness of its
> occurrence. (*DC*, 67, 69)

Still, we continue trying to see patterns and using terms like "fragment" that invoke nonexistent norms. While de Man contests the
legitimacy of this activity, he does not question its necessity: "No degree of knowledge can ever stop this madness, for it is the madness of
words" (*DC*, 68). If *The Triumph* shows that there are no answers, it also
shows that we have to continue asking questions, recuperating texts

and events in a process that "repeats itself regardless of the exposure of its fallacy" (*DC*, 69).

Rajan's interpretation is close to de Man's and so can be dealt with more briefly. She, too, notices the shimmering imagery of the poem and the unanswered questions. For her, the "Shape all light" recalls Alastor's dream vision, Intellectual Beauty (in "Hymn to Intellectual Beauty"), and many other similarly elusive figures in Shelley's poetry. Shelley cannot decide whether the Shape is real or illusory, an external presence or an imaginative projection that reality (symbolized by the procession) necessarily overtakes. Instead of resolving the ambiguity of the Shape, the poet remains in an energizing state of doubt and half-knowledge, neither renouncing the imagination and its creations nor trusting them. "Shelley's final poem is not logocentric" (it does not confidently attribute objective truth to the Shape), "yet it manages to triumph over its own deconstruction of a visionary poetics" (95) (it does not recant the need for fiction and the hope for correspondence between art and reality). The poem's discovery of the fictiveness of some fictions triggers the production of what turn out to be more fictions.

The open-endedness of *The Triumph* brings Rajan to look again at the apparent victory of idealism or logocentricism in some of Shelley's other works, most notably *A Defence of Poetry*. Here she finds a skeptical "subtext" at odds with the affirmative "official" text; the seemingly positive "text" originates in and tries to compensate for an anxious "subtext" it can never wholly overcome. Wishing to assign a cognitive function to poetry, the *Defence* describes poetry as withdrawing a "dark veil" from the spirit that resides at the heart of things beneath the superficial ugliness of daily life. Poetry, however, is also a "figured curtain," a "perfect and consummate surface" that does not so much uncover beauty as add beauty to a world that lacks it. Whether beauty is a "literal fact" (an external referent) or a "purely figurative construction that points behind itself to the dark ground of the figure, seems less certain than Shelley will allow" (28). Similarly, poetry is an active, transforming force, "a sword of lightning" and "the light of life." Yet it is also a passive mirror, teaching "self-knowledge and self-respect." While the mimetic side of Shelley wants to ground poetry in the external world, the prophetic side expresses (in Rajan's words) "impatience with subservience to present fact, and must also argue that poetry is an expressive outward projection of the golden world within" (74). The result is "the impossible concept of a mirror that has the power actually to transform what it reflects into the ideal" (74). "The disjunctive presence of a realistic poetics alongside a visionary poetics marks 'A Defence of Poetry' as a sentimental text, which engages in strategies of self-avoidance to escape being consumed by its own contradictions" (74–75). *The Triumph of Life,* by contrast, foregrounds the tensions that the *Defence* and other works (especially *Prometheus Unbound*) seek to hide. Shelley's last poem accordingly "'psychoanalyzes' and finally subsumes and overcomes its predecessors" (60).

If Rajan agrees with de Man in finding unresolved tensions in *The Triumph,* she derives these tensions from historical circumstances rather than from language. In a rather tangled critique of de Man, she argues that deconstruction is appropriate only to those texts which contest their own assertions. "There are, in other words, logocentric poems" (17, n. 6)—but not in the romantic period (or, apparently, in the nineteenth and twentieth centuries). De Man misconstrues the deconstructionist drive in romantic poems by attributing it to all poems. Similarly, he misunderstands the logocentric, self-mystifying side of romanticism, the side that resists deconstruction. He sometimes accuses the romantics of bad faith; he sometimes makes them more committed to self-irony or self-demystification than they actually were; and he sometimes suggests, in Rajan's words, that the "tendency of Romanticism to relapse into illusions it sees through" is also "something inherent in language, which cannot deconstruct except in relation to something constructed" (21–22, n. 14). Rajan sees the romantics' resistance to deconstruction as "something specific to Romanticism: an upsurge of the idealistic impulse, rather than simply an intermission in the drama of irony" (22, n. 14). In her view, this "upsurge of the idealistic impulse" sets off the romantics from their more consistently ironic modernist successors, just as a self-deconstructive tendency separates the romantics from their unequivocally logocentric predecessors. Rajan, in short, brings to her study of romanticism a respect for historical differences that she finds missing in de Man. The stalemate between logocentricism and deconstruction in *The Triumph of Life* is specifically romantic, not the constant product of language.

If nothing else, reviewing these interpretations of *The Triumph of*

Life should indicate the complexity of critical disputes. As I noted in chapter 3, critical disagreements are so difficult to resolve because no simple appeal to the evidence or to the rules of criticism decides them. Instead of supporting an interpretation, the evidence requires interpretation. And the rules of criticism are the subject of debate, not a clear-cut way of judging it. Absolute certainty is consequently impossible in interpretation and endless discussion to be expected.

The evidence accompanying the interpretations of the critics I have been discussing includes quotation, the genre of the poem, Shelley's other writings, and prior assumptions about poetry and romanticism. All of this evidence is legitimate; none of it speaks for itself. Further complicating—some would say weakening—the arguments of these critics are appeals to intangibles like tone (cf. Abrams on the "verve" of Shelley's writing in *The Triumph*) and personality (according to Bloom, Shelley did not mention Coleridge or Wordsworth in his poem because he was "too tactful and urbane to thus utilize those who were still, technically speaking, alive" [104]). Values and feelings are also at work in all these readings. When Abrams chides his contemporaries for reading their own despair into romantic poetry, he is not only interpreting romantic literature but offering it as an antidote to what he sees as an even more dispirited age than the one that the romantics addressed.

Despite the softness of their evidence and the contested status of their critical procedures, all the critics I have mentioned, "revisionist" and "canonical," agree on several points. First, they all call *The Triumph of Life* a fragment, left unfinished by Shelley's death. Some (de Man and Bloom) go on to question the completeness of other poems, but all agree that Shelley did not finish this one. Second, as far as I can tell, they all use the same edition of the poem, the one established by Donald Reiman in *Shelley's 'The Triumph of Life,' A Critical Study*. Acknowledging that the history of the poem's composition and publication is "complex," de Man still calls this edition "authoritative" (*DC*, 69, n.1). Third, these critics treat Rousseau in the poem as a reference to the historical Jean-Jacques Rousseau. This figure may also stand for Wordsworth and suggest other meanings, but on one level he is the author of *The Social Contract, Julie,* and other works with which we know Shelley was familiar. In de Man's words, "Shelley, an assiduous reader of Rousseau at a time when he was being read more closely than he has been since, evokes an ambivalence of structure and of mood that is indeed specifically Rousseau's rather than anyone else's, including Wordsworth's" (*DC*, 46–47). Fourth, these critics all see in the poem allusions to Wordsworth, especially to the "Immortality" ode. In de Man's terms, the "manifest presence" of Wordsworth in the poem is unmistakable (*DC*, 50). Fifth, these critics all see the structure of the poem as a skeptical series of questions and a "chain of metaphorical transformations," again to use a phrase of de Man's (*DC*, 58). Sixth, these critics all call the poem a dream-vision, which, until it is abruptly broken off, follows the "usual pattern" of such poems (Rajan, 69). Seventh, they all see parallels in imagery, structure, and theme between this poem and Shelley's other works. As early as 1948, Carlos Baker saw that "most of Shelley's poems [including *The Triumph of Life*] feed into one another."[6] No one has disagreed.

The originality of the revisionist critics I am examining, their claim to arrive at what Hartman calls "a better understanding and higher evaluation" of this poem, consequently does not rest on their disputing what I think we can call the basic facts about the poem (that it is a fragment, a dream-vision, etc.). Instead of contesting these facts, Bloom, de Man, and Rajan offer novel explanations of the point of these facts, their reason for being in the poem.

I find their explanations implausible. As I have already suggested, virtually everyone has noticed references to Wordsworth in this poem and has supposed that Shelley is continuing the quarrel with Wordsworth that he began as early as *Alastor* and "To Wordsworth." Writing well before what Hartman calls the "Revisionist Reversal" in criticism, Carlos Baker termed the poem "not a palinode against [Shelley's] previous affirmations about the poet's aspirations towards divine fire, but rather a palinode against Wordsworth's reluctant acceptance of what Shelley (and even Wordsworth) would regard as a lesser substitute."[7] Bloom differs from Baker and his other predecessors in the reason he gives for Shelley's reservations about Wordsworth, not in noticing tension between the two. In Bloom's view, Shelley criticizes Wordsworth's ideas about politics and nature because they are Wordsworth's, not because Shelley disagrees with them.[8] He has to curtail Wordsworth's influence in order to feel that he has something distinctive to say.

The problem with this reading is not that it fails but that it is foolproof. Nothing in the text can disprove it. One cannot object, for instance, that Shelley nowhere admits that his poem is a self-defensive battle with Wordsworth, or that Shelley's ideas about poetry emphasize cooperation rather than competition among poets (in the *Defence* he calls all poems "episodes of that great poem, which all poets, like the co-operating thoughts of one great mind, have built up since the beginning of the world"). Bloom can reply that Shelley's silence proves his point. Shelley is so "obsessed" with Wordsworth that merely mentioning his name would touch off anxieties of indebtedness that he could not control. Wordsworth's hold on him is so powerful that if he admitted what he was doing, he would fail.

But the fact that Shelley does not admit that he is self-protectively fighting Wordsworth hardly proves that he cannot admit it. The ultimate independence of Bloom's interpretation from anything in the text appears most vividly when he draws on other works by Shelley for support. First, he cites some well-known lines from *Adonais,* Shelley's elegy for Keats, which assert that

> From the contagion of the world's slow stain
> He [Adonais] is secure, and now can never mourn
> A heart grown cold, a head grown gray in vain;
> Nor, when the spirit's self has ceased to burn,
> With sparkless ashes load an unlamented urn.

In talking about old age, emotional depletion, and spiritual exhaustion, "it is still clearly Wordsworth and Coleridge that Shelley has in mind" (103)—more precisely, their ceasing to be "strong poets"—even though he seems to be talking more generally about the changes from which Adonais is now exempt. In this same poem Shelley also refers to "carrion kites that scream below" and says "He [Adonais] wakes or sleeps with the enduring dead; / Thou [the carrion kites that preyed on Adonais] canst not soar where he is sitting now.—" Again, in Bloom's opinion, Shelley is chiding Wordsworth and Coleridge (the "carrion kites") even though nearly every scholar thinks that Shelley is getting revenge on the reviewers whom he links to Keats's premature death. Finally, Bloom quotes the entire last paragraph of the *Defence,* with its famous concluding two sentences: "Poets are the hierophants of an unapprehended inspiration; the mirrors of the gigantic shadows which futurity casts upon the present; the words which express what they understand not; the trumpets which sing to battle, and feel not what they inspire; the influence which is moved not, but moves. Poets are the unacknowledged legislators of the world." Bloom's reading of this passage has to be seen to be believed:

> Unquestionably, the poets of whom Shelley is speaking here are not himself, Byron, and Keats, but primarily Wordsworth and secondarily Coleridge. . . . Wordsworth is a hierophant or expounder of the mysterious, even though he himself cannot apprehend what he expounds. Wordsworth is a transumptive mirror of futurity, and sings Shelley on to the battle of poetry long after Wordsworth himself is uninspired. And then comes the beautifully summarizing formula: Wordsworth is the unmoved mover, as an *influence*. The famous, much misinterpreted last sentence, "Poets are the unacknowledged legislators of the world," clearly needs to be interpreted in the context of the paradox that Shelley himself calls poetic "influence." . . . An unacknowledged legislator is simply an unacknowledged influence, and since Shelley equates Wordsworth with the *Zeitgeist,* it is hardly an overestimate to say that Wordsworth's influence created a series of laws for a world of feeling and thinking that went beyond the domain of poetry. Very strong poet that he was, Shelley nevertheless had the wisdom and the sadness of knowing overtly what other poets since have evaded knowing, except in the involuntary patterns of their work. Wordsworth will legislate and go on legislating for your poem, no matter how you resist or evade or even unconsciously ignore him. (110–11)

These examples from *Adonais* and the *Defence* show that Bloom's reading of *The Triumph* does not depend on the obvious allusions to Wordsworth that everyone finds in the poem. Bloom can discover Shelley struggling with Wordsworth anywhere, even (or maybe especially) in those texts which appear to be about something else. The *Defence* speaks of legislation and influence, to be sure, but of the influence of poetry on society, not of one poet on another. It is futile, however, to challenge Bloom's reading with references to the text because his interpretation does not require the poem's corroboration. Like Derrida in the exchange with Searle analyzed earlier, Bloom cannot lose; but because his reading cannot be falsified, it also cannot be proved.

Bloom is finally making a point that he cannot rationally defend; hence his vehement rhetoric (which tries to substitute hectoring for persuasion), his recourse to words like "unquestionably," "clearly," and "of course" (which circumvent the arguments he cannot make), and his touchiness when challenged (which shows up in his tendency to divide his readers into friends and enemies, bestowing excessive praise on the former and vilifying the latter). Bloom's interpretation of *The Triumph* derives from a theory of poetry that he brings to the poem, not from anything in the poem.

Most critics have observed that *The Triumph of Life* "seems to be shaped by the undoing of shapes" (to borrow a phrase of de Man's), but de Man is the first to make "the senseless power of positional language" (*DC*, 64) responsible for the poem's succession of metaphors. The appearance of language in de Man's argument, however, is too forced to be convincing. Signs of strain appear in his uneasiness with some of the details of the poem. First, if the Shape were to dramatize the tyrannical power of language over Rousseau, it would have to act on his mind with an "increased violence that erases the initial tenderness" (*DC*, 58). De Man rightly sees that the Shape progresses from gliding along the water to trampling the thoughts of her observer. But he overlooks these lines:

> "And still her feet, no less than *the sweet tune*
> *To which they moved*, seemed as they moved to blot
> The thoughts of him who gazed on them. . . ."
>
> (ll. 382–84; my emphasis)

The effect of the Shape is hypnotic and cumulative, not violent and sudden. Like a "sweet tune," she gradually dulls the consciousness of her observer by prolonging rather than erasing her "initial tenderness."

Similarly, if the triumph of life were to signal the triumph of language, then it would be fitting that a "rigid, stony arch" appear with the triumphal procession. The rigidity of the arch would bring to our attention the medium of language, the "figurality" of all signs, including the rainbow that first appears with the Shape. The masonry of the arch would make us see what we thought we could see through. Unfortunately for de Man's reading, though, the second rainbow (the rainbow that appears with the procession) is simply a rainbow. There is nothing "stony" or "rigid" about it. Shelley calls it "a moving arch of victory" which the "vermillion / And green and azure plumes [not bricks] of Iris had / Built high over her wind-winged pavilion . . ." (ll. 439–41). Failing to find a suitably solid arch in the poem, de Man has built one.

More importantly, if the impact of the Shape on Rousseau were to represent the force of language, then it would be appropriate if a change in sound were to accompany the Shape's "increased violence." It would be especially convenient if "the silver music" that first accompanies the Shape gave way to a steady, drumlike beat. Then one could conclude (as de Man does) that the poem is factoring out rhythm ("mere Measure") from song and clinching the association between the Shape and language ("accentual or tonal punctuation" being the common denominator of music and "spoken diction"). But while the beat may change, the song does not stop. I quote the entire passage, underscoring what de Man ignores.

> "And her feet, *ever to the ceaseless song*
>
> "Of leaves and winds and waves and birds and bees,
> And falling drops moved in a measure new
> *Yet sweet,* as on the summer evening breeze
>
> "Up from the lake a shape of golden dew
> Between two rocks, athwart the rising moon,
> Dances i' the wind, where never eagle flew.—
>
> "And still her feet, *no less than the sweet tune*
> To which they moved, seemed as they moved, to blot
> The thoughts of him who gazed on them. . . ."
>
> (ll. 375–84)

Even when the Shape moves "in a measure new," she does not interrupt the melodious music that surrounds her. She moves "ever to the ceaseless song" of nature, the "sweet tune" that constantly accompanies her. The reduction of "music to the mere measure of repeated articulations" takes place in de Man's essay but not in Shelley's poem.

De Man sees only language in control of *The Triumph of Life* because he already thinks that language is omnipotent. He refuses to let the poem challenge his prior assumptions. In a footnote on Shelley's judgment of the "Shape all light," de Man tips his hand: "It is perhaps naive to decide on a clear valorization on this level of rhetorical complexity; one would have to determine for what function of language the shape is a figure before asking whether an alternative to its function is even conceivable" (*DC*, 71, n. 4). I take de Man to be asking of the poem, What function of language does the Shape represent? not, Does the Shape represent a function of language? The poem does not have a chance; with a little tinkering, it plays back the assumptions about language de Man feeds into it.

Shelley, to be sure, was concerned about language and often commented on the difficulty of describing the silent, "imageless" "deep truth."[9] Perhaps his most famous complaint about his medium occurs in "Epipsychidion":

> . . . Woe is me!
> The winged words on which my soul would pierce
> Into the height of Love's rare Universe,
> Are chains of lead around its flight of fire—
> I pant, I sink, I tremble, I expire!
>
> (ll. 588–91)

But language for Shelley is finally a means, not a master. For all its inadequacy, language is still

> a more direct representation of the actions and passions of our internal being, and is susceptible of more various and delicate combinations, than colour, form, or motion, and is more plastic and obedient to the control of that faculty of which it is a creation. For language is arbitrarily produced by the imagination, and has relation to thoughts alone; but all other materials, instruments, and conditions of art, have relations among each other, which limit and interpose between conception and expression. The former is a mirror which reflects, the latter is a cloud which enfeebles, the light of which both are mediums of communication.[10]

Language differs from other media in degree, not kind. The fact that words are arbitrary combinations of letters and sounds is in their favor; it puts them closer to thoughts than more palpable media like "colour, form, or motion." Nevertheless, language is still a medium. "Language itself is poetry," Shelley says earlier in the *Defence,* suggesting that words are metaphors which put supersensible ideas in concrete form, as Shelley himself does when he says that language is a mirror or medium. He seems less dismayed, however, than de Man by the metaphorical status of statements. The necessity of figuring forth the truth, of finding signs for what cannot be literally or directly said, sometimes frustrates Shelley (as in "Epipsychidion") but never makes him despair. For him, language can be a "vitally metaphorical" way of marking "the before unapprehended relations of things and [perpet-

uating] their apprehension."[11] From Shelley's point of view, de Man
hardens a difficulty (imaging the deep truth) into an impossibility and
turns an opportunity (creating appropriate metaphors) into a dead
end. As Hartman himself admits, de Man's view of Shelley is "too
absolute" (*CW,* 108).

In arguing that historical conditions contribute to unresolved tensions in *The Triumph,* Rajan's reading is closer to my own than Bloom's
or de Man's. Like her (and virtually everyone else who has written on
the poem), I find the central occurrence of the poem to be Rousseau's
submission to the procession of Life. Rousseau's fate does not seem to
me desirable. He warns Shelley not to emulate him ("If thou canst,
forbear / To join the dance which I had well forborne!"); he is
disfigured; and the company he keeps includes popes, priests, and
tyrants, some of Shelley's most despised foes. Good may come of
Rousseau's fall but has not yet in the poem. And if anyone benefits
from what has happened to him, it will be Shelley (and the reader),
not Rousseau himself. His personal decline seems irrevocable.

Establishing the role of the Shape all light in Rousseau's downfall is
the basic problem posed by *The Triumph.* The Shape may be an agent
of the awful charioteer, an evil enchantress who dazzles Rousseau and
then offers him a sinister drink. Or the Shape may represent possibilities of resistance to the procession that Rousseau fails to pursue,
perhaps because he skeptically questions her ("Show whence I came,
and where I am, and why—"), perhaps because he forsakes her when
the procession appears.

I agree with Rajan that the function of the Shape remains uncertain. Rousseau, it is true, tends to blame himself, not the Shape or the
procession, for his fate. He tells the narrator,

> "I feared, loved, hated, suffered, did, and died,
> And if the spark with which Heaven lit my spirit
> Earth had with purer nutriment supplied,
>
> "Corruption would not now thus much inherit
> Of what was once Rousseau. . . ."

(ll. 200–204)

He hints at neglected options:

> ". . . I among the multitude

> Was swept—me sweetest flowers delayed not long;
> Me not the shadow nor the solitude;
>
> "Me, not that falling stream's Lethean song;
> Me, not the phantom of that early form
> Which moved upon its motion,—but among
>
> "The thickest billows of the living storm
> I plunged, and bared my bosom to the clime
> Of that cold light, whose airs too soon deform."
>
> (ll. 460–68)

Still, Rousseau's language is ambiguous. The passive voice ("I among the multitude was swept," "I was laid asleep") indicates subjection to forces beyond his control. More importantly, the Shape all light whom he blames himself for deserting is only a "phantom of that early Form" he encountered before the procession, "a ghost" more dim "than a day-appearing dream,"

> The ghost of a forgotten form of sleep;
> A light of heaven whose half-extinguished beam
>
> Through the sick day in which we wake to weep
> Glimmers, forever sought, forever lost. . . .
>
> (ll. 427–31)

The vagueness of the Shape makes her presence questionable: she may only seem shadowy and unreal to a person caught up in everyday life; or she may be a mirage, "forever sought, forever lost." Transcending the procession remains a tantalizing but obscure possibility in this poem—more obscure than Abrams's admittedly tentative reading will allow.[12] Shelley's desire for release or redemption is clearer than his means of obtaining it. He wants to blame Rousseau but has difficulty showing that Rousseau had a choice, that "purer nutriment" would have made any difference in his life.

The incompleteness of the poem matches a lack of resolution in Shelley's other works (here again I agree with Rajan). In general terms, Shelley's doubts center on the political and cognitive claims he wants to make for poetry. He wants to call poetry an instrument of knowledge and social change, but he is not sure how he can substantiate such a claim. His work consequently resounds with unanswered questions about the objective truth of the imagination (see the often quoted last three lines of "Mont Blanc"), unheard pleas for political

influence (in, for example, "Ode to the West Wind"), and an unresolved conflict between longing to escape society and longing to influence it (especially prominent in the conclusion of "Lines Written
Among the Euganean Hills"). Shelley's wavering between confidence
and despair, activism and retreat, never stops; his doubts, as Rajan
observes, are terminal rather than intermediate.[13]

Historical conditions contribute to Shelley's uncertainty without, of
course, fully accounting for it. David Erdman, E. P. Thompson, Carl
Woodring, and Raymond Williams (among others) have described
these conditions, and I will not review their analyses in detail here.
Put very simply, political and intellectual isolation helped produce the
insecurity and aggressiveness—the aggressiveness born of insecurity—that inform Shelley's writing. Raymond Williams's comments on
the romantic artist seem especially pertinent to Shelley. On the one
hand, Williams notes "obvious elements of compensation" in the romantic defense of poetry: "at a time when the artist is being described
as just one more producer of a commodity for the market, he is
describing himself as a specially endowed person, the guiding light of
common life." Yet, Williams continues,

> this is to simplify the matter, for the response is not merely a profes-
> sional one. It is also (and this has been of the greatest subsequent
> importance) an emphasis on the embodiment in art of certain human
> values, capacities, energies, which the development of society towards
> an industrial civilization was felt to be threatening or even destroying.
> The element of professional protest is undoubtedly there, but the
> larger issue is the opposition on general human grounds to the kind of
> civilization that was being inaugurated.[14]

Sustaining this opposition in the absence of political and intellectual
support (in Shelley's case, censorship, exile, and ridicule) proved
understandably difficult, and "the difficulty was not solved, but
cushioned, by an idealization"—by tributes to poetry even greater
than those which initially triggered the poet's self-doubt. "The last
pages of Shelley's *Defence of Poetry*," Williams concludes, "are painful
to read. The bearers of a high imaginative skill become suddenly the
'legislators', at the very moment when they were being forced into
practical exile; their description as 'unacknowledged', which, on the
theory, ought only to be a fact to be accepted, carries with it also the
felt helplessness of a generation."[15] In protesting too much that poetry

is important, Shelley is trying to convince himself as well as his age. Perhaps, he seems to be hoping, a firm persuasion that poetry is indispensable will make it so. An undercurrent of wishful thinking, of which Shelley is sometimes aware, at once generates and unsettles his exorbitant praise of art.

If by and large I agree with Rajan's interpretation of Shelley, I nevertheless dissent from her evaluation (and here I turn to Hartman's claim that revisionist critics have arrived at a "higher evaluation" as well as a "better understanding" of the romantic writers). Rajan goes to great lengths to assert her love of the romantics. In a remarkably candid statement, she admits that at first she did not think very much of them: "Unlike the Romantics, who consented to be educated in illusion before they discovered its limitations, I began with an automatic sense of irony toward a group of poets whom I assumed to be sensitive only to daffodils" (9). After some time, however, she learned "to recognize that the Romantics were more modern than I had thought, and that their refusal to cross the threshold into modernism was a choice and not a failure" (9). She owes this insight to Milton Wilson: "his undergraduate course on the Romantics taught me to respect a group of poets whom I had intended as victims of my deconstructive energies" (9).

Still, for all Rajan's admiration of these poets, she cannot help sounding disappointed when their works hesitate to self-deconstruct. Her comment on Shelley's *Defence* is typical of several other remarks in her book: "The disjunctive presence of a realistic poetics alongside a visionary poetics marks 'A Defence of Poetry' as a sentimental text, which engages in strategies of self-avoidance to escape being consumed by its own contradictions" (74–75). Similarly, she says of Blake, Wordsworth, and Coleridge,

> Although a historical discussion of the evolution of Romanticism has not been one of my purposes, it seems appropriate to conclude by suggesting that such an evolution did occur. The early Romantics are characterized by a more unbending commitment to a transcendental poetics, by a reluctance to follow through on their own insights, and most significantly, by the absence of that radical irony which makes it impossible to turn back to illusion. (265)

Rajan may not think she is criticizing these writers, but I find her talk of escape, evasion, repression, reluctance, self-mystification, and avoidance quite damaging. She certainly cannot be applauding the romantics for failing "to follow through on their own insights" and relapsing into "illusion." Elsewhere, the generosity she shows these poets tends to patronize them. She excuses their self-mystification by referring to their historical context, much as neoclassical critics explained Shakespeare's "barbarism" by citing the influence of his ignorant audience. Rajan's negative verdict (romantic literature is unsophisticated) overshadows her expression of tolerance (the poets are not to blame but their deluded age).

Rajan's condescension toward these writers is at odds with her more valuable emphasis on their uncertainty. Far from regressing into illusion or consenting "to be educated into illusion," these poets were not sure that the correspondence between art and reality is necessarily illusory. After stressing their indecisiveness, Rajan acts as if they knew the falsity of their claims for art and then escaped or repressed that knowledge. After empathizing with these poets' courageous self-doubt, she makes them out to be cowards.

An optimistic view of history, as insidious and complacent in its judgment of past writers as Enlightenment theories of progress, mars Rajan's appreciation of romanticism. In her view, the more recent, the better, that is, the closer to the truth; hence the differences between the early and the late romantics, Shelley's early work and his last poem, romanticism and modernism. Unlike the romantics themselves, she knows their aspirations for art are fictions, forever dead because they seem not to have survived in the work of some contemporary critics.

The judgments that Bloom and de Man make of Shelley similarly fail to do him justice. Bloom calls *The Triumph* Shelley's "greatest achievement" (98) and Shelley a "superbly intelligent," "very strong" poet (111): "he knew that he could not escape the shadow of Wordsworth, and of and in that knowing he made his own poetry" (111). And de Man credits *The Triumph* with an especially "rigorous" understanding of language. In particular, he defends Shelley's imagery, often found "incoherent and erratic," for its "extraordinarily systematic" presentation of the inexorable workings of language (*DC*, 57). Both critics seem to me to compliment a poem Shelley did not write. If excellence depends on knowingly swerving from a precursor or "thematizing" the "positional power of language," then the author of *The Triumph of Life* was a poor poet. He did neither.

In some ways Bloom, de Man, and Rajan read *The Triumph of Life* correctly; in other ways, however, they misread it. In my view, their insights occur despite their commitment to indeterminacy, while their errors occur because of it. In Rajan's case, I see nothing specifically deconstructionist about her admirable interpretation of *The Triumph of Life*. In treating the poem as the historical act or "choice" of an individual agent rather than as an illustration of a preexistent theory of language, she is successfully challenging a critic like Abrams on Abrams's own grounds. But if her command of the poem owes nothing to deconstruction, her condescension toward the poem reflects the disinclination or inability of deconstruction to question its own assumptions.

Similarly, when de Man and Bloom are right about the poem, it is despite the fact that their readings do not seem to need the poem. When they are wrong, it is because they feel free to read into the poem prior commitments—Bloom to his theory that all poets self-defensively misread the predecessors who influence them, de Man to his theory that all texts dramatize the inexorable operation of language. My point here is not simply that Bloom and de Man make mistakes in their interpretations, but that their respective theories of interpretation provide no criteria for criticizing their errors. Convinced that all readings are misreadings, Bloom is disposed not to correct his misreading but to strengthen it, making it even more perverse (or less "idealistic"). Persuaded, like Miller, that all shapes attributed to a text distort it, de Man is not simply free to tamper with the details of the poem; he thinks that he must tamper with them in order to say anything about the poem at all. Instead of posing a problem, the imposition of critical will over a text becomes a necessity, even, in Bloom's poetics, a virtue.

In reviewing these discussions of *The Triumph of Life,* I have shown that critics as diverse as de Man, Bloom, Baker, and Abrams agree on several points. I do not wish to put too much weight on the fact that these different critics can agree. In particular, I am not using the agreement of these critics to prove that the poem is coherent or that it permits only one reading. Questions remain about the poem (for example, does the Shape trap Rousseau or offer possibilities of transcendence that he fails to seize?); there are many valid things to say about it; and we cannot be absolutely certain about even those points on which de Man and the others concur. In observing where these interpretations overlap, I do not claim, then, to have explained all the poem or even to have uncovered its "core" or "center."

Nevertheless, if it would be naïve to make too much of critical agreement, it would also be naïve to dismiss it as compliance with merely arbitrary constraints. At the very least, the agreement of these otherwise antithetical critics should make us question the deconstructionist's persistent treatment of texts as enigmas, labyrinths, or tangled webs of meaning. Judging from the readings that I have been discussing, I think we can say that some poems—even an admittedly elusive poem like *The Triumph of Life*—present an experience that competent readers can share.

I have been questioning the alleged undecidability of literary works, in chapter 3 faulting the theories that advance this idea and in this chapter objecting to the misreading that it enables. As I noted earlier, the indeterminacy of texts is not just a theoretical issue but, in poststructuralism, a practical means of demystifying what recent critics see as oppressive academic conventions. Borrowing a phrase of Derrida's, in my next chapter I accordingly turn to "the deconstruction of a pedagogical institution and all that it implies."

V

"The deconstruction of a pedagogical institution and all that it implies": Poststructuralism and Academic Criticism

As I stated in my introduction, disenchantment with academic criticism partly inspires deconstruction and explains its appeal. In skeletal form, the argument of revisionist critics looks like this:

1. Academic criticism depends on ideas of competence, agreement, and correctness in interpretation. The typical academic critic, in this view, is the teacher grading papers or the editor considering a manuscript, each confidently winnowing out error and certifying some readers as better (more "professional") than others.
2. Critics as different as the New Critics and Northrop Frye defended correctness in interpretation, thus inspiring curricula and text-books and otherwise earning the favor of the academy.
3. Competence, however, is a repressive fiction undermined by the "force" of writing, or the resistance of writing to any meaning or pattern imposed on it.
4. Because revisionist critics seek to release rather than tame this force, their work is therefore anti-institutional, the target of scorn and ridicule from the academic establishment that it threatens.

In this chapter I want to flesh out this argument first by defining what deconstructionists mean by academic criticism and then by showing how they use the indeterminacy of texts against what they regard as its narrowness. I go on to demonstrate why this attack on the academic profession fails, resulting in the assimilation of revisionist criticism by the institution that it wants to oppose.

By "academic critics," American deconstructionists have in mind their immediate precursors in the academy, the New Critics and Northrop Frye. In this view, the New Criticism earned its hegemony in the university, first, by defining literature as a special use of language and, second, by making literary criticism a teachable discipline grounded in the recovery of verifiable meanings from texts. The New Criticism, in short, gave the teaching profession what it needed (and presumably still needs): a teachable method and a distinctive subject matter, individual literary works.

By emphasizing archetypes, Frye broke down the New Critics' isolation of the literary work, anticipating one of the deconstructionists' leading ideas. By deriving these archetypes from literature as a whole, he shifted attention from the individual poet to the grammar of the human imagination—the rules that all authors heed in making literary works. And by making literature as a whole a matrix of imaginative possibilities from which all verbal constructs derive their shape, Frye put literature at the center of human culture. Finally, by extending romanticism, by recovering the projection of myths of concern on things as they are, Frye abandoned the self-contradictory attempts of the New Critics to claim some truth of correspondence for literature.

From a deconstructionist point of view, although Frye accordingly went far, he did not go far enough in challenging the New Criticism: hence Hartman's gibe, quoted earlier, that Frye's theory offers "the most liberal theology or justification of art the modern professional has managed to devise." Although Frye overcame the autonomy of the discrete poem, he nevertheless continued to claim independence for literature as a whole, which he, like the New Critics, opposed to extraliterary writing. For him, moreover, the self-contained realm of literature, like the self-enclosed poem in the New Criticism, displays a minutely organized "real structure," which the critic can map. As Frye observed in the *Anatomy*,

> Criticism as knowledge, the criticism which is compelled to keep on talking about the subject, recognizes the fact that there *is* [Frye's emphasis] a center of the order of words. Unless there is such a center, there is nothing to prevent the analogies supplied by convention and genre from being an endless series of free associations, perhaps suggestive, perhaps even tantalizing, but never creating a real structure. . . . If there are such things as archetypes at all, then, we have to take yet another step, and conceive the possibility of a self-contained

> literary universe. Either archetypal criticism is a will-o'-the-wisp, an
> endless labyrinth without an outlet, or we have to assume that litera-
> ture is a total form, and not simply the name given to the aggregate of
> existing literary works.[1]

Not an "endless labyrinth without an outlet" or "center," literature is a
"total form" that critics can progressively chart, making criticism a
means of "scientific" knowledge. Valuing clarity, detachment, progress, knowledge, and other pedagogical virtues in criticism, Frye's
theory, in this view, does not simply tolerate institutionalization but
embraces it, finding its home in the university, which presumably
safeguards the freedom that articulateness brings. As he notes in *The
Great Code,* "all my books have really been teachers' manuals, concerned more with establishing perspectives than with adding
specifically to knowledge."[2] Instead of making new discoveries, Frye,
like a certain kind of teacher, has been interested in organizing,
clarifying, and popularizing what he thinks we already know.

Deconstructionists rupture Frye's "self-contained literary universe"
as well as the New Critics' autotelic poem. In deconstruction, irony
corrodes the point of rest that, for the New Critics, ostensibly ends it
(for all its irony, ambiguity, and paradox, the poem in the New Criticism is still a structure of resolved stresses, "balancing and harmoniz-
ing," in Cleanth Brooks's phrase, "the apparently contradictory and
conflicting elements of experience by unifying them into a new pattern"[3]). Literature as a whole, in turn, merges with "writing," an endless maze of differences that disrupts any order imposed on it. And
criticism gets sucked into the maelstrom that it pretended to survey
from afar. Literature, criticism, extraliterary discourse, even reality—
these categories, upheld by the New Critics and Frye, become in deconstruction differences, marks that run together in the seamless web
of textuality.

The capacity of writing to undo the distinctions that it encourages
is, in deconstruction, its "force." As Hartman explains,

> It [the "priority of language to meaning"] expresses what we
> [presumably the contributors to *Deconstruction and Criticism*] all feel
> about figurative language, its excess over any assigned meaning, or, put
> more generally, the strength of the signifier vis-à-vis a signified (the
> "meaning") that tries to enclose it. Deconstruction, as it has come to be
> called, refuses to identify the force of literature with any concept of
> embodied meaning and shows how deeply such logocentric or incar-

nationist perspectives have influenced the way we think about art. . . .
Commentary, the oldest and most enduring literary-critical activity, has
always shown that a received text means more than it says (it is "allegor-
ical"), or that it subverts all possible meanings by its "irony"—a rhetorical or structural limit that prevents the dissolution of art into positive
and exploitative truth. (*DC,* vii–viii)

Deconstructionists claim, then, that they make interpretation a means
of releasing, instead of throttling, the force of literary works, turning
criticism into a risky, liberating venture—as creative, powerful, and
free of determinate reference as literature itself.

Instead of effacing ourselves before the text and what it signifies,
we should, in this view, celebrate our own inventiveness, the "text"
and its signified being two of the many creations that we have mistak-
enly reified. In "Interpreting 'Interpreting the *Variorum,*'" Stanley
Fish expressed the release that results from the dissolution of seemingly "positive truth" into arbitrary fiction:

> the fictions of formalism [that there are right readings authorized by
> the text] have the disadvantage of being confining. My fiction [that all
> interpretive strategies are arbitrary] is liberating. It relieves me of the
> obligation to be right (a standard that simply drops out) and demands
> only that I be interesting (a standard that can be met without any
> reference at all to an illusory objectivity). Rather than restoring or
> recovering texts, I am in the business of making texts and of teaching
> others to make them by adding to their repertoire of strategies.[4]

Fish has subsequently repudiated this statement, calling it "the most
unfortunate" he ever wrote (*TC,* 174). In *Is There a Text in This Class?*
he notes,

> The only thing that drops out in my argument is a standard of right
> that exists independently of community goals and assumptions. Within
> a community, however, a standard of right (and wrong) can always be
> invoked because it will be invoked against the background of a prior
> understanding as to what counts as a fact, what is hearable as an argu-
> ment, what will be recognized as a purpose, and so on. (*TC,* 174)

Nevertheless, despite this change in his position, Fish detects "something of the police state in [M. H.] Abrams's vision [of texts with
determinate meanings], complete with posted rules and boundaries,
watchdogs to enforce them, procedures for identifying their violators
as criminals" (*TC,* 337). Although revised to take into account the

pressure of community norms, Fish's argument somehow remains "liberating": holding readers accountable to the preexistent meaning of a text still smacks of tyranny.

If nothing else, the supposition that texts are indeterminate has unleashed some furious writing, aimed, like Fish's statement, at freeing interpretation from spurious controls. Instead of whispering their results to their neighbors, as Keats advised, recent critics are more prone to shout them at their enemies: "the class police," "the Graffs and the Hirsches of this world," who terrorize interpretation with "the night-stick of verification and the handcuffs of validity";[5] "Hebrew, Athenian, Roman, Christian, European, and finally American and Russian imperialism" and its "idea that Truth is One— unambiguous, self-consistent, and knowable";[6] "the murderous fictions of our history," all of them inspired by the "rush to the referent . . . [and] the insider's deluded hope for truth";[7] and, more generally, "truth, value, and rationality" and the "structures of domination" that they necessitate.[8] In all these comments, interpretation has become what Gayatri Spivak terms a free fall, intoxicating us with "the prospect of never hitting bottom." Tapping the feelings of release, adventure, and danger that fuel much recent critical writing, Spivak goes on to hail deconstruction as "a way out of the closure of knowledge. By inaugurating the open-ended indefiniteness of textuality—by thus 'placing in the abyss' *(mettre en abîme)* as the French expression would literally have it—it shows us the lure of the abyss as freedom."[9]

It would be truer to what might be called the anguish of deconstruction to say that interpretation *could* be a free fall, were it not for the false bottoms that the academic profession puts between critics and the abyss. The immediate target of the vehement rhetoric that I have been citing is consequently the university, for American poststructuralists the "police state" closest to home.

After leveling reading to more or less strong misreading, Bloom, for example, bitterly observes that competence in interpretation is an oppressive delusion:

> One of my most instructive memories will be always of a small meeting of distinguished professors, which had gathered to consider the qualifications of an individual whom they might ask to join their enterprise. Before meditating upon this person's merits, they spontaneously

> performed a little ritual of faith. One by one, in turn, they confessed
> their belief in the real presence of the literary text. It had an existence
> independent of their devotion to it. It had priority over them, would be
> there after they were gone, and above all it had a meaning or meanings
> quite apart from their interpretative activity. The literary text was *there.*
> Where? Why, in editions, definitive editions, upon which responsible
> commentaries might be written. Responsible commentaries. For "re-
> sponsible," substitute what word you will, whatever anxious word
> might match the social pieties and professional civilities that inform the
> spirituality of such occasions. (*DC,* 8)

For "responsible" we might substitute reasonable, true, authoritative,
probable, legitimate, and even interesting. Bloom pictures the insecure professors reassuring each other of their correctness and exclud-
ing dangerous outsiders in the name of arbitrary norms ("he goes too
far," "her analysis isn't as complete as his," etc.).

Bloom sees himself as one of these outsiders. By arguing that "there
is always and only bias, inclination, pre-judgment, swerve," he has
exposed what his less self-aware colleagues presumably repress.
Hence the latter's angry, defensive reaction:

> By defining poetic strength as usurpation or imposition, I am offend-
> ing against civility, against the social conventions of literary scholarship
> and criticism. But poetry, when it aspires to strength, is necessarily a
> competitive mode, indeed an obsessive mode, because poetic strength
> involves a self-representation that is reached only through trespass,
> through crossing a daemonic threshold.[10]

Bloom transgresses against the "social conventions of literary scholarship and criticism" because they are only social. There are no "responsible commentaries": the "professional civilities" of academic life mask
a power struggle among more or less strong misreadings.

Despite Hartman's differences with Bloom—in his opinion, "*misreading* is a wrong-headed term, more spirited than helpful" (*CW,*
52)—he, too, chafes under "academic" criteria of objectivity and proof.
Recently a reader (Spencer Hall) objected that an article of Hartman's
violates "rules of evidence and argumentation," multiplies "needless,
arbitrary, or self-indulgent complexities," oversteps "the bounds of
evidence and common sense," and wallows in "obstructive, opaque,
and esoteric jargon." Hartman replied by impugning the vagueness and
undesirability of Hall's norms:

> . . . Hall's call for law, order, and proper argument has its own question-
> able assumptions that, to my mind, depress literary studies today. . . .
> What if the game of criticism has changed, or the rules of the game are
> being questioned? Even if that were not so, do we want critics to be
> certified by a Normal School? . . . Not our subjectivity is to be feared
> but our overreaction to it, those pseudo-objective criteria which im-
> prison both the work and ourselves.[11]

With characteristic ambivalence, Hartman does not so much want to
abandon these criteria as to supplement them. As a teacher he admits
that interpretation has a "service function" that he does not want to
destroy. "Teaching, criticizing and presenting the great texts of our
culture are essential tasks" (*DC*, vii)—even though criticism devoted to
these chores and the illusory standards of correctness that they imply
becomes uninteresting.

So do the critics themselves, especially the "academy-grown variety," who end up victims of a psychology of "deepening dependence" before the texts and professional hierarchies that they serve:

> It is not an exaggeration to say that the critic has become a retainer to
> those in our society who want not the difficult reality but merely the
> illusion of literacy: if he practices in an English department, he carves
> and trims and patches and binds the prose of future leaders destined
> to build or destroy the economy; and if he becomes a journalist or
> reviewer he flatters, cajoles and admonishes the authors of books
> whose profits keep the publishers happy and his own job relatively
> secure. . . . The criticism that restricts itself to the elucidation of par-
> ticular texts, and defines what is literary in the narrowest formal terms
> [Hartman means here the New Criticism], is indeed a trade, and does
> not leave the area of specialization it enriches. . . . [The critic] accepts
> too readily his subordinate function. He denies that he has a "psychol-
> ogy" worth considering, or, to put it differently, he represses his own
> artistic impulses. (*CW,* 215, 216)

Hartman sometimes writes as if he expects only drudgery from criticism that prostrates itself before educational purposes. In his opinion,
the "advent of mass education," which seems irreversible, has made
the "pedagogic and socializing function" of criticism "immeasurably
increased and burdensome." Teachers, moreover, comply with their
own "humiliation": "because of classroom pressures and an adminis-
trative structure that treats them as a business," they support the
"journalistic leveling of their function to one thing: direct, saleable

communication." Things are bad but Hartman is hopeful. Although the "basement" of literary study may be forever "service-ridden," critics are still "free to fall upwards" by renouncing in their writing the constraints that hobble them when they grade papers, attend tenure meetings, and teach. Criticism today is "particularly vital" because it is doing just that. Without repudiating its service function, it is reclaiming "its free-lance, creative powers" and becoming art (*CW,* 238, 257).

Derrida is less cautious. Like Hartman, he scorns readers who hold him accountable to "academic" norms. In "Border Lines," for instance, he mocks a "feminist leader" who calls one of his hypotheses "mad": "she [Derrida later names her Miss Blind] used the most academic criteriology against me, demanded 'proof,' and so on" (*DC,* 166–67). And he implies that as a writer he indulges in freedoms that he cannot take as a teacher:

> This operation [superimposing one text on another, which he does throughout "Living On"] would never be considered legitimate on the part of a teacher, who must give his references and tell what he's talking about, giving it its recognizable title. You can't give a course on Shelley without ever mentioning him, pretending to deal with Blanchot, and more than a few others. And your translations have to be readable [cf. Hartman's "direct" and "saleable"], that is, in accordance with criteria of readability very firmly established, and long since. ("Border Lines," *DC,* 84–85).

Derrida, however, goes further than Hartman and equates the conventions of literary study with the rules that govern—and repress—society as a whole. The demand for truth in texts, for example, becomes the fiat of doctors, policemen, and judges as well as professors who, like detective Joe Friday, want nothing but the facts. These authorities

> demand an *author,* an *I* capable of organizing a narrative sequence, of remembering and telling the truth: "exactly what happened," "recounting facts that he remembers," in other words saying "I" (I am the same as the one to whom these things happened, and so on, and thereby assuring the unity or identity of narratee or reader, and so on). Such is the demand for the story, for narrative, the demand that society, the law that governs literary and artistic works, medicine, the police, and so forth, claim to constitute. (*DC,* 98)

This police-minded demand for truth—for authors who take responsibility for what they say—finds reinforcement in other fictions: copyright laws, strictures against plagiarism, contracts, and other expressions of the institution of private ownership. Reading for truth becomes an exemplary act of economic and technological mastery; when we claim to know what a text says, we possess it, consume it, even rape it.

Some critics of Derrida, most notably Frank Kermode, have objected that communication, despite its indeterminacy, takes place according to conventions that they concede are arbitrary. But Derrida's target is the illegitimacy of these conventions, not their workability. These rules work but only because when they are about to break down—when a student, say, snaps at a teacher, "that's just your opinion," or a defendent tells a judge, "who's to say what's larceny?"—"the police is always waiting in the wings."[12] Administrators, department chairmen, employers, and troops are always already prepared to force the rebel in line—"always already" because "conventions are by essence violable and precarious, *in themselves* and by the fictionality that constitutes them, even before there has been any overt transgression. . . ." ("LI," 250). Force takes over where reason fails, as in interpretation it must.

For Derrida, writing is the undetected time bomb ticking beneath literary study, the university, the economy, the legal system, and other seemingly solid structures. When we hear the ticking—when Derrida and others force us to notice it—we presumably clutch all the more anxiously at the conventions that muffle it (as Hartman accuses Hall of doing in the exchange I have cited). Teachers can always add another text to their reading lists—even *Das Kapital*—but they supposedly cannot accommodate textuality, which overruns the distinctions they have to keep in place.

> A politico-institutional problem of the University: it, like all teaching in its traditional form, and perhaps all teaching whatever, has as its ideal, with exhaustive translatability, the effacement of language [*la langue*]. The deconstruction of a pedagogical institution and all that it implies. What this institution cannot bear, is for anyone to tamper with [*toucher à;* also "touch," "change," "concern itself with"] language, meaning *both* the *national* language *and,* paradoxically, an ideal of translatability that neutralizes this national language. Nationalism and universalism. What this institution cannot bear is a transformation that leaves intact

neither of these two complementary poles. It can bear more readily the
most apparently revolutionary ideological sorts of "content" if only
that content does not touch the borders of language [*la langue*] and of
all the juridico-political contracts that it guarantees. It is this "intolerable" something that concerns me here. ("Border Lines," *DC,* 93–95)

Deconstructing the fiction that writing is a transparent, passive
medium—and doing so "not merely in a theoretical manner"—should
be the aim of anyone who "does not want the police to be omnipotent"
("LI," 251).

The charges that the deconstructionists make against the New
Critics, Frye, and academic critics in general have alarmed many
readers. The New Critics and some of their sympathizers, for instance, are convinced that Derrida et al. have discarded their ideas.
Murray Krieger echoes the sentiments of Cleanth Brooks, W. K. Wimsatt, and René Wellek when he notes "how thoroughly all vestiges of
that old New Criticism have been swept away by the new wave of our
newer criticism, dominated by recent continental influences."

> As he [J. Hillis Miller] shows us, recent critical fashions in the academy
> have sprung forth from assumptions that altogether preclude those of
> the New Criticism, thereby denying us their methods of literary analy-
> sis and the considerable fruits which such methods could bear. If our
> newer new criticisms go as Miller sees them going, then all continuity
> with earlier criticism in our century is severed, and we must unsay
> some rich decades of critical saying.[13]

Other commentators on recent theory fear the destruction of
academic criticism that deconstruction seems to promise. In the critique of Hartman I have already mentioned, Spencer Hall expresses
the common worry that while "critics like Hartman have opened up
exciting new possibilities," their assumptions about writing "threaten
the very existence of literary studies." And, with even less hesitation,
Peter Shaw calls deconstruction "degenerate criticism," a symptom of
the "dismal state of English studies," which are on the verge of declining to "the current marginal status of the classics." Deconstructors are
preparing literary study for "inconsequence"; they are digging their
own graves.[14]

But the academic establishment has not collapsed before revisionist
criticism; it has scarcely trembled. Esteemed journals like *PMLA*
routinely publish deconstructions of various texts; the esteem of great

Western writers like Shakespeare, Milton, and Wordsworth remains undiminished, indeed augmented, as deconstructors show that these writers realized the heterogeneity of their own writing;[15] and the argument from authority persists, though critics now are more likely to call on Derrida, Foucault, and de Man than Frye or Brooks when making a point in a scholarly article or evaluating colleagues and job candidates. A few years ago William Schaefer, then the editor of *PMLA*, observed, "At times . . . it seems that authors feel their articles would not be given serious consideration without a quotation from Frye, preferably in the opening paragraph." Schaefer's successor, Joel Conarroe, found out that things had changed when he took thirty-five essays submitted to the journal and tallied the number of essays that cited various critics (the essays had survived two specialist readings and were being considered by the *PMLA* editorial board, so they were well regarded). Derrida came in first (ten papers mentioned him), followed by Barthes (seven), Miller (six), de Man (five), Bloom (four), and Hartman (four).[16] For all its talk of upending hierarchies, poststructuralist criticism, in short, has given new names to old ones, relegating "direct, saleable communication" to the "basement" (to use Hartman's words) and equating self-deconstruction with vitality.

There are theoretical as well as institutional reasons for this continuity. Despite their professed uneasiness with the formalism of the New Critics and Frye, deconstructionists take to an extreme one of its cardinal assumptions, namely, that literary texts do not represent some referent that explains or justifies them.[17] Most of the New Critics, to be sure, asserted that literature offers genuine knowledge and that objective analysis aids our understanding of a poem. But the extrarational terms in which they defined poetry prompted the New Critics themselves to warn against trying to seize in prose the experience of a poem. These warnings backfired: intended to save poetry from reduction, they clouded the truth in the poem they tried to protect. Here, for instance, is Cleanth Brooks on the heresy of paraphrase:

> If we are to get all these qualifications into our formulation of what the poem says—and they are relevant—then, our formulation of the "statement" made by Herrick's poem will turn out to be quite as difficult as that of Pope's mock-epic. The truth of the matter is that all such formulations lead away from the center of the poem—not toward it; that the "prose-sense" of the poem is not a rack on which the stuff of

the poem is hung; that it does not represent the "inner structure" or
the "essential" structure or the "real" structure of the poem. We may
use—and in many connections must use—such formulations as more
or less convenient ways of referring to parts of the poem. But such
formulations are scaffoldings about the building. We must not mistake
them for the internal and essential structure of the building itself.[18]

In what may be as good a motto as any for deconstruction, Derrida
observes that "once quotation marks demand to appear, they don't
know when to stop" (DC, 76). In Brooks's statement, the quotation
marks that enclose "prose-sense" invade the center that he wants to
defend.

When Brooks talks skeptically of what a poem "says," "states,"
"means," "communicates," and so forth, he only wants to deny that
readers can rationally restate the meaning of a poem. Anxious to
avoid reduction, he falls back on tautology: only the poem says what it
says. The poem that he isolates, however, resembles writing as Derrida describes it: severed from genre and authorial intent, abandoned
to the norms of language, its meaning leads a secret life outside what
readers say about it. Frank Lentricchia reports that "too many genera-
tions of students came out of New-Critical classrooms convinced that
their teachers possessed knowledge of the 'hidden' meanings of texts
to which there was no systematic and disciplined access."[19] One can see
why from Brooks's view that discursive formulations take us away
from the core of meaning that they claim to describe. For deconstructionists, the hidden, "internal and essential" meaning of the poem is a
charade that elites perpetrate to keep outsiders (here, students) in
their place. Already in Brooks a shadowy presence beyond rational
discovery, the center is reinserted in the chain of differences it supposedly orders. The scaffolding of interpretation, to use Brooks's
metaphor, extends the sprawl of the building (the poem).

The New Critics' skeptical theory of literary meaning, in short,
foreshadows the deconstruction of their truth claims for criticism and
poetry. Similarly, the deconstructionist assault on Frye in fact extends
him, turning his theory against itself. Frye's assertion that even discursive writing owes its form to literature becomes in deconstruction the
crack that opens his self-contained literary universe. As mentioned
earlier, Frye complicates but does not eliminate access to objective
truth when he acknowledges that the myths and metaphors we find in
literature shape all verbal structures, including, one must suppose,

literary criticism. In commenting on this assumption, I proposed turning the continuity of literary with extraliterary writing to the cognitive advantage of literature. Deconstructionists take the opposite tack, arguing that the ineluctable fictiveness of discursive structures keeps them from becoming truthful assertions. The myths that literary critics, say, impose on their data falsify the interpretations that result—unless there is some rational way of validating myths, and for Frye there is not (if there were, myths would not be myths). Frye's appeal to objective truth, in criticism and elsewhere, becomes groundless or, at the very least, unearned.

Ostensibly "detached" discourse is, in this view, always already "concerned" (to use Frye's terms). Our access to reality blocked, the tension that Frye posits between reality and literature gives way, in deconstruction, to the tension between writing and the texts that it contains. In Harold Bloom's terms, texts fight for their own space before they interpenetrate; individual writers, whether critics or poets, try vainly to author the forms that their works displace. "In literary as in human romance," Bloom remarks, "there is an anguish of contamination, a sense of being impinged upon by all rival romances. A prose or verse romance always fights to get free of the verbal universe that nevertheless it is condemned to join." Frye, he concludes, is the "seer of that joining, but not of the poetic will's struggle to be free."[20] Bloom explains in psychological terms what de Man, Derrida, and Miller attribute to language, but all four critics try to account for much the same thing. For all these critics, a text lengthens the chain of signifiers that it tries to end, even a text that aims at representing an external signified, whether the objective world or "the real structure" of a literary work.

For these critics, then, the lack of reference that for Frye characterizes literature also applies to criticism, not to mention the social sciences and the other extraliterary avenues to objective truth that Frye wants to keep clear. Even as poststructuralists accordingly go beyond Frye, they also, again, extend a line of thought that Frye initiates. Instead of demolishing Frye's system, deconstructionists let it tumble, the fictiveness of the patterns that inform extraliterary writing having already rendered inevitable the system's collapse.

Despite the antipathy of deconstructionists to formalism, deconstructionists are thus as eager as the New Critics and Frye to avoid the reduction of the literary work to "something other than it, toward a referent (a reality that is metaphysical, historical, psychobiographical, etc.) or toward a signified outside the text whose content could take place, could have taken place outside of language, that is to say, in the sense that we give here to that word, outside of writing in general." I am quoting Derrida, who goes on to say that "although [deconstruction] is not commentary"—that is, it does not simply aim at "doubling" the meaning or structure of the text—deconstruction nevertheless "must be intrinsic and remain within the text." Deploring the reduction of the text to an external signified, Derrida significantly opts for "intrinsic" reading, "intrinsic" of course being one of the code words of the New Criticism. Derrida rightly adds, however, that he prefers intrinsic reading "for more radical reasons" than those given by his predecessors. Extrinsic interpretation is not simply undesirable in literary criticism though possible elsewhere, say, in a discipline like history. The extrinsic reading of a text is always impossible, there never having been "anything but writing" "beyond and behind what one believes can be circumscribed as [a] text."[21]

Instead of repudiating formalism, deconstruction accordingly solidifies its basic tenet. No longer a heuristic option, the nonreferentiality of literature becomes a necessity: one cannot refer a text—any text—to something outside it if, as Derrida says, given "the absence of the referent or the transcendental signified," "*there is nothing outside of the text*" (his emphasis). Anxious to avoid reduction, the New Critics, again, fell back on tautology, allowing only the poem to say what it says. Equally anxious to read poetry intrinsically, deconstructionists favor what seems to me a superficial expansiveness. History, philosophy, and other kinds of writing, to be sure, may now enter literary study—but as literature, redefined as "writing." The openness that results is finally claustrophobic, as literary critics invite historians and philosophers to share their confinement in language. "Invite" is too polite a word: these other writers have no choice if, as J. Hillis Miller says, all efforts to escape the "prisonhouse of language" only build the walls higher. In this view, we—and I am speaking here of literary critics—can move into other disciplines; trace a literary text to its biographical, historical, and political context; and even abandon the interpretation of texts for other experiences. We can do all these things, moreover, without escaping textuality. "One can never escape from this labyrinth," Miller notes, "because the activity of escaping makes more labyrinth. . . ."[22] The apparently bold advances of deconstruction "beyond formalism" turn out to be steps on a textual tread-mill. These critics (to switch metaphors) break down barriers, transgress limits, and explore everywhere, knowing that they will never break the linguistic web that encloses them. Instead of escaping their specialty—the ostensible aim of their attacks on the New Critics and Frye—these critics thus magnify it and find freedom in its im-perialist expansion.

For all their hostility to the academic profession, revisionist critics consequently reflect well-established tendencies in the institution that they oppose. Nothing could be more academic or professional than their professed attack on the academic profession, which not only protects the autonomy of literature (i.e., its freedom from reference to a reality that other disciplines can investigate) but expands that autonomy at the expense of rival disciplines, turning them into exten-sions of itself. In a moment I will explain what I mean here by "academic" and "professional," but first I should note that other critics have sensed the harmony between the university and poststruc-turalism that I am describing. Christopher Ricks, for instance, conjec-tures that Harold Bloom's obsession with strength partly results from "the situation that George Bernard Shaw understood"—"that of a university-trained writer feeling he and his work are not somehow as manly as other men and their work, and, so Shaw says, wallowing 'in violence and muscularity of expression, as only literary men do when they become thoroughly depraved by solitary work, sedentary cow-ardice, and starvation of the sympathetic centers.' "[23] And Denis Donoghue derives the appeal of deconstruction partly from its attrac-tiveness

> to the clerisy of graduate students, who like to feel themselves superior to the laity of common readers, liberated, too, from the tedious re-quirement of meaning as such, the official obligation to suppose that words mean something finite rather than everything or nothing. De-construction allows them to think of themselves as forming a cell, the nearest thing the universities can offer in the form of an avant-garde. The wretched side of this is that deconstruction encourages them to feel superior not only to undergraduates but to the authors they are reading.[24]

There is some truth to both these explanations, but we can go further if we fill in the portrait of the academic profession that they sketch.

To grasp what it means to be "a professional," we must first under-stand that, while profit may justify other kinds of labor, a service ideal presumably motivates professionals and gives their work a disinter-ested appearance.[25] A self-imposed code of ethics binds members of a profession, the public supposing that only professionals are compe-tent to evaluate their peers. The professions in turn have won this freedom from public regulation by claiming that their work rests on a distinctive body of knowledge. Although theoretically accessible to anyone, this knowledge requires years of formal training, mostly at a university, during which students master the terminology and princi-ples that distinguish their career. They may be interested in learning for its own sake or for its social value, but their professional education will be rigorously competitive, relying on such incentives as grades, class rank, and financial aid. Advancement within a profession, like admission to it, continues up a hierarchy, with titles and rites of pas-sage marking the stages of ascent. Unlike many people, professionals can thus feel pride in their work. Extensive training, the approval of colleagues, and the trust of clients all certify the expertise of profes-sionals, and an ethic of service gives moral support to their success.

Although the professions have performed many beneficial func-tions, they have also abused the power that the public has given them. Under their veneer of service, they have often acted like other, less moralistic special interest groups (corporations, for instance) and con-fused their own well-being with the welfare of society as a whole. In psychological terms, the professions at their worst have enforced a self-serving, parochial outlook on their members, encouraging them to think that they do not work in a particular field but live for it. Especially when compared to other workers, professionals train so hard, enjoy so much freedom, get so much praise, and, in general, feel so important, that they have greater incentive to identify with their role than, say, a garbage man or a busboy. Dedication more easily turns into obsession and blind partisanship in professions than in other occupations. While avowing and sometimes heeding an ideal of public service, the professions, in short, have also encouraged self-centeredness. By equating competence with expertise, they have atomized knowledge, perpetuated dependency on their services, and legitimized the ambitions of individuals who allow their careers to override every other concern.

Since its inception in the eighteenth century, writing has been a profession even more ambiguous than most. On the one hand, imaginative writers and literary critics have seen themselves as professionals: motivated by high ideals (dedicated, in Arnold's phrase, to discovering and propagating the best that is known and thought in the world); bound by common values and truths (Shelley, for instance, saw all poems "as episodes to that great poem, which all poets, like the cooperating thoughts of one great mind, have built up since the beginning of the world"); and best equipped to judge each other's work. On the other hand, they have had difficulty earning these claims. From the outside, writers have appeared in a less flattering way: as entertainers using inflated rhetoric to camouflage their real function; as cantankerous egotists forever involved in pointless internecine disputes and petty jealousies; and, in general, as more or less successful businessmen trying like everyone else to make their way in the market and doing everything one would expect of people in their predicament—including making suspiciously grandiose claims for their "services." Or so writers have thought; in some ways, this view of public opinion was a convenient caricature—convenient because it rationalized disappointment and neglect.

In any case, contemporary academic critics would seem to have resolved the dilemma of their nineteenth-century predecessors. With the university between academic critics and the marketplace, they can publish books and articles that would never succeed commercially. Protected by tenure, academic critics can deal with unpopular ideas. Backed up by institutional requirements as well as the needs of their discipline, they can teach courses that few students would voluntarily take. Writing and teaching, to be sure, count toward advancement up the professional ladder. But unlike free-lance writers, academic critics do not live entirely off their writing. Unlike plumbers, they do not sell their services directly to clients. Academic critics would seem, in short, to have become complete professionals, people whose avocation is their vocation.

This rosy picture has never corresponded to reality, but in the 1950s and early 1960s it seemed on the verge of becoming fact. The university was rapidly expanding, and English teachers faced a new, insecure, ambitious audience partly made up of middle-class students many of whose parents had never gone to college. Baffled by difficult texts like "The Waste Land," yet lacking confidence in their judgment, these students were ready for experts to help them. A teacher's prob-

lem was not so much attracting or motivating students as simply training them; hence the preoccupation with method that distinguished
the leading critics of the day—the New Critics. The New Critics' purposes of course went beyond making Eliot, Donne, and Joyce intelligible to university students. But that was one way teachers used the
New Critics' ideas. In addition, as deconstructionists note, the New
Critics gave a growing profession a distinctive subject matter, literature, by arguing that poems were autonomous wholes whose nondis-
cursive use of language demanded that students read them in a
special way. Inculcating that way of reading became the teaching profession's service. Academic critics demonstrated their competence by
analyzing particular poems, evaluating them according to intrinsic
criteria, and passing on these skills to students. By formulating ax-
ioms like the intentional and affective fallacies and the heresy of
paraphrase, the New Criticism, in short, made interpretation appear
to be an objective discipline that students could systematically learn—
even students from diverse cultural, economic, and educational back-
grounds. Ignorance of literary history, unfamiliarity with other
disciplines, and crude philosophical assumptions were no handicaps
in analyzing the self-contained poem. Just as importantly, the New
Critics proved to these students what many of them already sus-
pected, namely, that they *had* to learn how to read. Reading a poem
differed from reading just about anything else, including philosophical, religious, political, historical, and scientific texts.

The list of what poems were not seemed endless. After the New
Criticism had so shielded its subject matter from the encroachments
of other disciplines, it was no longer clear to many what poems and
critical interpretations were for or how they related to our other
"extrinsic" concerns. The New Critics of course advanced great claims
for their work; they asserted that poems provide "complete knowledge" and that the "resuscitation of the humanities" was somehow
vital to society. But their dedication to the special integrity of poetry
undermined their support of these claims, which consequently remained abstract gestures rather than convincing statements of purpose. After confining criticism to textual analysis, the New Critical
teacher was always in the position of postponing a discussion of the
relevance of reading to another time and place—maybe in an ethics
or politics or philosophy class but not here, where we do literary
criticism. Sympathetic observers of the New Critics like Murray

Krieger have tended to give them the benefit of the doubt, seeing in their hesitation insuperable epistemological problems that originate in romanticism and continue to plague critics who try to claim cognition and autonomy for literature. But harsher commentators like Richard Ohmann (in *English in America*) have construed their humanistic claims as rationalizations, ideological poses that excused their "flight from politics" to the comfortable and harmless confines of the university. After the New Critics, criticism, in Ohmann's analysis, had become just another "bourgeois" profession, piously vowing service to humane values but actually existing for the sake of its practitioners. Despite the Arnoldian rhetoric with which the New Critics sanctified literary study, poems seemed to exist for the interpretations that they made possible; producing criticism in turn allowed critics to scale the professional hierarchy. The use of all this to society was less certain than its value to individual critics.

In my own view both Krieger and Ohmann are partly right: Krieger in describing the origins and intentions of the New Criticism, Ohmann in criticizing some of its effects. By restricting criticism to such narrow tasks, the New Critics rationalized its production but left it without any clear rationale. In retrospect, we can see that favorable conditions apparently having little to do with literary theory—like prosperity and a postwar baby boom—allowed the New Critics to take for granted the purposes of what they were doing. Writing in 1969, Frederick Crews could observe that

> much recent criticism has been characterized by a primness of tone, a spirit of dry routine, and a preoccupation with abstract formal patterns. The New Critics, with their generally nostalgic politics and their ostentatious piety, are usually blamed for this arid development, but the accusation is unfair, for most of the men who have been called New Critics were artists and thinkers with a clear sense of their commitments. The hallmark of most criticism produced today is precisely its low degree of commitment, its air of occupying a niche rather than of claiming some territory. The niche is the one where most of us reside— the affluent and multifarious university, the crowning ornament of a credit-card civilization whose basis cannot be examined with a clear conscience. Our obvious difference from the liveliest critics of thirty years ago is that we are completely at home in academe. And if the most general trait of recent criticism is its absence of worry over what the business and loyalty of the critic should be, this is because the answer is intuitively known: he should enter the academic hierarchy and do whatever it asks of him.[26]

Since 1969 the university has become more like a financially threatened government agency than an affluent home. Inflation and declining enrollments, among many other developments, have lessened the demand for teachers, especially in the humanities. A depressed job market has not made literary study in the university meaningless; it has, however, weakened a major aim of literature courses—to prepare students (mostly English majors) for a niche in the academic profession. The production of criticism continues, of course, but aimlessly, meeting no compelling need except professional necessity. In the absence of any sense of what criticism is for, quantitative standards of judgment take over, as if the sheer volume of criticism will somehow give it a point.[27]

Meanwhile, students understandably are losing interest in literature courses—the profession's hierarchy of rewards being closed to them—and many teachers and administrators are belatedly looking for ways of justifying an enterprise that appears moribund, sustained, if at all, by inertia. Unfortunately, many of these well-intentioned defenses of literary study are couched in the language of public relations—as if the plight of the humanities were an "image" problem that will go away once we find a more "credible" way of "promoting" and "packaging" what we do (I paraphrase here William Schaefer's well-known "Still Crazy After All These Years"). Putting the problem in these terms encourages the suspicion that it is not really a problem.

Recent criticism mirrors the profession it criticizes in part because it misreads the conditions I have been describing. The profession itself has already weakened—or failed to strengthen—the targets that Hartman, Bloom, and Derrida in particular attack. Hartman's complaint to the contrary, a "service function" does not weigh down our transactions with literature. As Arnold saw, the undemocratic, mechanical, and specialized character of industrial work makes aesthetic experience seem at best a palliative (the music that the dentist plays or the paintings that brighten the office) or at worst a frill (the symphony ticket that only the rich can afford). Even where literacy and the standard of living have improved, the dehumanizing conditions of work have remained. The arts still seem impractical—except for the artists, critics, publishers, museum directors, and dwindling number of professors who make a living off them—because work requires other skills, like the mindless acceptance of routine instead of creativity, or specialization instead of self-expression. In times of prosperity—like the 1950s and early 1960s in America—we have had more leisure and money for the arts, but their weekend status has stayed the same.

Understandably anxious about finding work now that the teaching jobs are scarce, students in literature courses are consequently not "future leaders destined to build or destroy the economy" (again to quote Hartman), or, if they are, it is not because they are taking English courses. The apparent irrelevance of literary study encourages critics to defy the constraints that Hartman thinks shackle them. As the audience for criticism shrinks in enthusiasm, numbers, and confidence each semester, jargon, recondite allusiveness, and aimless wordplay are more easily tolerated. Unlike a judge, say, whose interpretive decisions matter enough for others to debate and question them, the academic critic has little incentive to be clear, fair, or thorough. Because our decisions are inconsequential, we seemingly can afford to leave them to whim and chance. A profession unsure of its usefulness, in short, welcomes, or at least endures, the "unservile" writing that Hartman thinks it discourages.

In "The Perpetual Error," Angus Fletcher illustrates the lengths some readers will go to exonerate opacity. "Quite deliberately," Fletcher observes of de Man, "taking careful steps, one after the other, he creates a sort of functional obscurity," not because he cannot write but because language has died "as the natural medium of truth."[28] De Man cannot lose: his obscurity does not cloud his thesis but reinforces it. Now that criticism aspires to art, many of the strategies with which the New Critics justified murky writing in literature have come to the rescue of critical prose, another sign of the indebtedness of deconstructors to the critics they often attack. In my view, the audience for academic criticism is dying, not the truth-telling capacity of language. Hartman, in any case, chastises "direct, saleable communication" in interpretation at a time when few people are buying.

Similarly, when Derrida assaults "criteria of readability," he rips apart paper chains. These criteria have never been "very firmly established" in our profession: hence the need for a book like Jonathan Culler's *Structuralist Poetics*, which aims at clarifying what we mean by competence in criticism. In a system so uncritically given over to production, moreover, assailing these criteria may not be an "intolerable" effrontery, as Derrida thinks, but a precondition for further growth. As Gerald Graff observes,

> Where quantitative "production" of scholarship and criticism is a chief
> measure of professional achievement, narrow canons of proof, evi-
> dence, logical consistency, and clarity of expression have to go. To insist
> on them imposes a drag upon progress. Indeed, to apply strict canons
> of objectivity and evidence in academic publishing today would be
> comparable to the American economy's returning to the gold stan-
> dard: the effect would be the immediate collapse of the system. . . . The
> recent discovery that every text can be reinterpreted as a commentary
> on its own textual problematics or as a self-consuming artifact ensures
> that the production of new readings will not cease even though explica-
> tion of many authors and works seems to have reached the point of
> saturation.[29]

Textuality, which opens all texts to endless reinterpretation, does not
abolish publications but rather multiplies them, each text always allowing even more to be written "about" it. Derrida further accelerates
production by erasing the distinctions between literary and extraliterary works, subsuming everything in words under "writing." Instead
of transcending his specialty, as I said earlier, he underwrites its im-
perialist expansion, which fashionable "interdisciplinary" courses like
Literature and Business or Literature and Philosophy have already
begun by annexing the adjoining disciplines to the curriculum without disturbing, or rethinking, what we already have. Far from putting
an end to curricula, textuality describes how they usually grow, one
text, author, period, and genre adhering to another in a shapeless,
directionless mass.

My point about the production of criticism is less extreme than it
may first appear. I am not arguing that deconstructionists deliberately
seek to broaden the possibilities of critical production, or that paving
the way for new readings is all that deconstruction achieves, or even
that academic criticism needs deconstruction in order to grow. Releasing interpretation from the controls of proof and objectivity does not
so much increase the supply of the product as acquiesce in its aimless
growth, which is already going on full force without deconstruction.

Despite Bloom's worry (really a boast) that he offends "against civil-
ity, against the social conventions of literary scholarship and criticism," he, too, reflects the circumstances that he thinks he risks
challenging. Instead of fighting the atrophy of public interest in criticism, Bloom redeems the critic's isolation by assigning interpretation
private goals. In his theory, lack of respect for other authors is reborn
as creativity and strength; ambition, self-validation, and personal

freedom eclipse more generous reasons for writing. No longer a means of communication or discovery, interpretation becomes in theory what it sometimes is in fact: solely a means of individual advancement, of salvaging a place for oneself at someone else's expense. The current depression of the academic literary profession favors this shift to self, just as its earlier expansion encouraged the New Critics' self-effacing concern for the poetic object. In the absence of other ends, personal ambition seems to explain what critics do, tempting them to see even poetry itself as an arena of self-interested combat that legitimizes their own competition.

If it is wrong, then, to take the radical claims of revisionist criticism at face value, it is also wrong to dismiss them as so much nonsense. I share Hartman's impatience, for example, with narrow stylistic norms in interpretation and literature. When applied by enrollment-minded administrators and lazy or frustrated students, "common sense," "plain, ordinary language," and "clarity" can be suffocating standards. By recovering the complexity of literary works, Hartman properly unsettles our reliance on easy answers and challenges our accommodating literary study to torpid students. He champions a kind of writing that is rightfully more "speculative," "enthusiastic," "involuted," "oracular," "demanding," "personalized," "creative," "colorful," "eccentric," "playful," and "fun" than the bland messages that safely pass examination questions.[30]

But for Hartman all interpretations, not just some of them, "journalize" literature. At times he can describe writing as "a labyrinth, a topological puzzle and textual crossword; the reader, for his part, must lose himself for a while in a hermeneutic 'infinitizing' that makes all rules of closure appear arbitrary" (*CW*, 244). But "a while" turns out to be forever:

> As a guiding concept, indeterminacy does not merely *delay* the determination of meaning, that is, suspend premature judgments and allow greater thoughtfulness. The delay is not heuristic alone, a device to slow the act of reading till we appreciate . . . its complexity. The delay is intrinsic: from a certain point of view, it is thoughtfulness itself, Keats's "negative capability," a labor that aims not to overcome the negative or indeterminate but to stay within it as long as is necessary. (*CW*, 269–70)

"As long as is necessary" modulates to as long as possible: although Hartman realizes that "forms of closure will occur" in interpretation

(*CW,* 270), no form of closure should occur. The purpose of the "critical essay today" is therefore not "merely to illustrate or reinforce a suppositious unity but to show what simplifications, or institutional processes, are necessary for achieving any kind of unitary, consensual view of the artifact" (*CW,* 196–97). Authority in interpretation is only a pretense, a spur of the moment or habitual invention, necessitated by institutional pressures and won by purging the text of complexities that can never be mastered (*CW,* 22).[31]

I have already suggested in chapters 3 and 4 why I think that this view of interpretation is misguided. Put simply, Hartman, like Derrida, jumps from the impossibility of passing a definitive "last judgment" on a reading (*CW,* 239) to the impossibility of rationally evaluating a reading. If Hartman's theory were correct, then his only alternative to "routinizing" literary works would seem to be leaving them alone. Instead of shoring up distinctions between forced and legitimate readings, Hartman finds expediency, blindness, and coercion behind any "consensual view of the artifact," thereby undermining his trenchant critique of some views. In the absence of any defensible way of mastering texts, the only means of removing them from "the danger of being routinized or contaminated by endless readings forced out of the industrious hordes of students" (*CW,* 230) would seem to be not to teach literature courses—an option that many universities are already pursuing, as the "hordes of students" in literary study dwindle to a handful. Taken to its logical conclusion, Hartman's defense of indeterminacy harmonizes with the stratagems of the bureaucrats he rightly criticizes.

Similarly, the departmental meeting satirized by Bloom, in which professors cling to each other and expel outsiders in the name of bogus norms, is not a fiction. But when Bloom asserts that "there is always and only bias, inclination," he sabotages his own protest, leaving us only the choice between more or less successful impositions of power. The professors he derides are more concerned about their own careers than with the complex truth, but instead of remedying their arbitrariness, Bloom's epistemology makes it inevitable. The other side of his bitterness is futility.

Finally, Derrida rightly mocks the objectivity of many rules and detects the brute force beneath their reasonable façade. When he leaps from the arbitrariness of some conventions to the illegitimacy of them all, however, he, too, neutralizes his own complaints. No longer directed at a specific kind of politics, his argument discredits "all ethical-political statements," even those which aim at changing the conditions that he deplores. Derrida states his opposition in terms that make acting on it impossible; he protects himself against failure by insuring it. Angry but helpless, he settles for irony and self-deprecation (putting words like "truth" and "reality" in quotation marks to show that he does not take them seriously, or mocking the scholarly conventions, like footnotes, which he nonetheless heeds). His furious rhetoric culminates in parodying what he feels helpless to refuse or change.[32]

Perhaps because revisionist criticism exudes helplessness, its references to politics are often hopelessly vague. The following passage from Hartman is typical:

> No wonder some are scared witless by a mode of thinking that seems to offer no decidability, no resolution. Yet the perplexity that art arouses in careful readers and viewers is hardly licentious. It is the reality; it is only as strange as truth. It recalls the artificial nature or purely conventional status of formal arguments or proofs; the fact that human agreements remain conveniences with the force of law, metaphors with the force of institutions, opinions with the force of dogma. It recalls the prevalence of propaganda, both in open societies that depend on conversation, jawboning, advertising, bargaining, and in controlled societies that can become sinister and inquisitorial, adding to their torture chamber the subtlest brainwashing and conditioning devices without giving up the brazen and reiterated lie. Can any hermeneutics of indeterminacy, any irony however deeply practiced and nurtured by aesthetic experience, withstand either society while they are still distinguishable? (*CW,* 283)

Failing to mention any specific human agreement, institution, argument, or opinion, this passage indicts them all, leaving the impression that the distinction between open and controlled societies is itself artificial or cosmetic, like the difference between advertising and brainwashing, both forms of propaganda. The threat that both societies supposedly pose to art overrides their other differences. Specific political and economic references are accordingly missing in this passage because there does not seem to be any reason to bring them up. The adventitious status of all human agreements eclipses any distinctions we might want to make among them. Instead of complementing political involvement, Hartman's talk of mastery and emancipation apparently substitutes for it, expressing desires that political action cannot satisfy while leaving oppression and inequality untouched.

More consistently than Derrida, who can speak of "'literatures' or 'revolutions' that as yet have no model" ("LI," 243), J. Hillis Miller acknowledges the "conservative aspect of deconstruction" that I am emphasizing here:

> Its difference from Marxism, which is likely to become more sharply visible as time goes on, is that it [deconstruction] views as naive the millennial or revolutionary hopes still in one way or another present even in sophisticated Marxism. This millenarianism believes that a change in the material base or in the class structure would transform our situation in relation to language or change the human condition generally. Deconstruction, on the other hand, sees the notion of a determining material base as one element in the traditional metaphysical system it wants to put in question. . . . Deconstruction does not promise liberation from that famous prison house of language, only a different way of living within it.[33]

Trapped in the prison house of language, we are helpless to study the world, much less to affect it. I am consequently not sure what Miller's unspecified "different way of living" could be. Anxious to show that deconstruction is not destruction, he leaves its impact unclear.

Whereas a critic like Frye allows for knowledge (of the record of history and so on) and for progress (through the lessening of intolerance), Miller and Derrida turn even these oases into mirages created by the sequential drift of words, which use us even as we claim to use them. For deconstruction, the tragic irony that Frye sees in revolution undercuts all our attempts to master history. As de Man notes in "Shelley Disfigured," "nothing, whether deed, word, thought or text, ever happens in relation, positive or negative, to anything that precedes, follows, or exists elsewhere, but only as a random event whose power, like the power of death, is due to the randomness of its occurrence" (DC, 69). In this dire view, arranging to meet someone for lunch is as "naïve" as hoping to "change the human condition generally."

In criticizing Miller and the other writers discussed in this chapter, I am not denying that argument in interpretation can (and often does) disguise coercion, bias, dogmatism, habit, and other reasons for arbitrarily deciding on a reading. My point is that if every transaction between a teacher and student, say, must be an imposition of power, then there is no way of criticizing force—much as if sexual love were always rape, then it would be sentimental to oppose rape. In my view, we can distinguish between force and persuasion, indoctrination and education, change and progress, societies that thwart and nurture the self. A typical deconstructionist move undoes these admittedly value-laden distinctions by implicating the first term in the second—which is why I find deconstruction deeply conservative and cynical. By "conservative" I do not mean a principled resistance to change but a skeptical disbelief in the possibility of improving things in any way, improvement suggesting a false way out of the endless play of differences in which language supposedly traps us.

In this chapter I have been disputing the picture of academic criticism that makes an attack on the determinacy of texts seem radical. In this view, academic literary study resembles a "police state" with rigid prohibitions against playful, colorful, freewheeling interpretations. These prohibitions are backed up by a firm belief in the possibility and desirability of extracting verifiable meanings from literary works, the correct interpretation of literary texts being the humiliating "service function" imposed on critics by students, administrators, and the larger public. Revisionist critics unmask these meanings as frauds, invented in part to validate the exclusion of allegedly incompetent outsiders or to insure their inclusion on the basis of their learning the "right" way to read.

Instead of this picture, I see something quite different: an uncertain, anxious, isolated profession willing (or forced) to tolerate the experimentation that Hartman and others think that it proscribes. In my view, revisionist critics attack readability in interpretation at a time when few people outside the academic profession are reading criticism; they deride the "service function" depressing literary criticism when literature courses (if not expository writing courses) lack a clear rationale; and they scorn "academic criteriology" (proof, truth, evidence, and so on) in circumstances already conducive to expediency and cynicism.

I have argued in chapters 3 and 4 that the skepticism about language that motivates deconstruction is unwarranted. Here I have been trying to show that it is also costly. By maintaining that progress (whether intellectual or political) cannot occur, deconstructionists guarantee that it will not occur. The assimilation of deconstruction by the academic profession reflects the tameness, even the redundancy, of deconstruction, a remedy that perpetuates the ills it seeks to cure.

VI

Does Deconstruction Make Any Difference?

In this book I have been trying to link three topics often kept separate: Matthew Arnold and Northrop Frye's defense of poetry; the attempt of deconstructionists and others to show that literary texts are indeterminate; and the currently troubled state of academic literary study. The line that I have been tracing from Arnold and Frye through deconstruction and academic criticism takes many turns. By distinguishing literature from extraliterary writing (including criticism), by making literary study a source of moral values ("ideas of perfection" in Arnold, "myths of concern" in Frye), by allowing for reference to reality in detached or discursive writing (if not in literature), by encouraging the institutionalization of their critical principles, and by affirming the possibility of progress, Arnold and Frye resist deconstruction: hence the desire of some critics to use their work as an answer to deconstruction. Arnold and Frye, however, also anticipate deconstruction by dispensing with truth claims for literature, thereby weakening what they set out to defend—most importantly, the moral authority of literature and the cognitive status of discursive writing, especially literary criticism. Instead of demolishing these defenses of poetry, deconstruction abets their self-destruction by pulling the already loose thread that jeopardizes them.

In linking Arnold and Frye to deconstruction, I have been laying down several conditions that a successful defense of poetry must meet. By "a successful defense," I mean one that justifies the importance of literature to our other intellectual, practical, and aesthetic concerns—our need for conduct and our need for beauty, as Arnold put it. To defend literature we must, first, defend its truth claims, or its capacity to enlighten what we do when we are not reading. Second, political action must help remove the obstacles in the way of literature, among them inequality and the degradation of work. Claiming a vocational function for literature depends on nothing less than humanizing work, organizing work as well as leisure around the values that literature can sanction.[1]

Elsewhere I hope to show that a defense of poetry can meet these conditions. Here, however, I have been demonstrating that failure to satisfy them keeps literature peripheral. I have also been questioning the arguments advanced by deconstructionists and others against the referentiality and determinacy of literary texts. Often directed at the insularity, tedium, and aimlessness of academic literary study, these arguments reinforce what they set out to dismantle. Conditions in the academic profession favor the theorizing that revisionists think the academy discourages; hence the absorption of revisionist criticism by the established order that it wishes to defy.

In seeing deconstruction as a self-nullifying attempt to free interpretation from the confines of academic criticism, I am suggesting an analogy between the shortcomings of Arnold and Frye and the shortcomings of deconstruction. These projects not only are at odds with themselves for many of the same reasons—in particular, their uneasiness with the cognitive status of literature—but they ultimately aim at the same goal: the extension of human freedom. Deconstructionists, to be sure, regard as a barrier the separation of criticism from literature that for Frye "liberates the works of culture themselves as well as the mind they educate." But deconstructionists assail Frye not out of wanton destructiveness but out of a genuine (if abortive) desire to protect human freedom, Frye's overriding concern.

Unlike some critics of deconstruction, then, I do not dismiss its talk of liberation as so much hot air. Unlike many partisans of deconstruction, however, I do not take its radical rhetoric at face value. Contemporary critics are addressing real problems, albeit in confused and self-destructive ways. In concluding, I want to refine this view of deconstruction by looking at two texts that seem to me symptomatic of larger tendencies in the work of Derrida, Hartman, and the other critics that I have been discussing: Christopher Norris's *Deconstruction Theory and Practice* (1982), a sympathetic study of Derrida and his

American critics and advocates, and J. Hillis Miller's "The Function of Rhetorical Study at the Present Time" (1979), an application of deconstruction to the curriculum.

Despite the vast commentary on deconstruction, it is admittedly still difficult to determine whether Derrida and his American allies expect practical results from their theorizing, whether, as I have been urging, they seek to make a difference in the way we treat works of literature. As in any movement that has met with vitriolic opposition, the claims of deconstructionists reflect the often fierce accusations that these critics are answering. When self-described "conservative" or "traditionalist" opponents equate deconstruction with terrorism, the decline of the humanities, and the destruction of traditional values, many advocates of deconstruction emphasize its ludic, purely pleasurable fascination with the free play of language and the subtleties of "slow reading." The charge that the movement is dangerous thus generates the reassuring, often bemused reply that it is not nihilistic, destructive, and so on.[2]

Still other critics of deconstruction pounce on this defense as an admission of failure. For them, deconstruction is consequently the irresponsible pastime of jaded, escapist professors at elite universities, securely beyond the erosion of budgets, writing skills, and enrollments. To refute the charge that deconstruction is harmless, sympathizers urge that much more is at stake than the entertainment of a few professors—in fact, everything from the revival of literary criticism to political freedom. What looked at first like a child's toy turns out to be a real tool for tearing down repressive conventions and building a new kind of literary criticism.

At first glance, Norris exemplifies this second way of defending deconstruction. In *Deconstruction Theory and Practice*, he attributes enormous power to deconstruction, calling it in his introduction a technique for "making trouble" and "the active antithesis of everything that criticism ought to be if one accepts its traditional values and concepts."[3] He repeatedly praises its "unsettling power" (70), "exhilarating spirit" (92), and "liberating force" (21). In his account, deconstruction is tirelessly on the move, challenging, unmasking, combating, attacking, unfixing, undercutting, shaking, dislodging, wrenching, breaking down, defying, questioning, transforming, undoing, disturbing, undermining, annulling, unsettling, dismantling,

collapsing, transgressing, opposing, resisting, subverting, and invert-
ing. The targets of all this "perverse," "devastating," "dangerous,"
"sinister," "disconcerting" activity are nothing less than "every normal
and comfortable habit of thought" (xi), "everything that criticism
ought to be if one accepts its traditional values and concepts" (xii),
"the whole traditional edifice of Western attitudes to thought and
language" (29), "age-old conceptual limits" (57), "every last vestige of
philosophic truth and certainty" (77), "the normative constraints of
effective communication" (113), "the solemn conventions of Anglo-
American academic discourse" (113), and "all proprietory limits"
(114).

It should not be necessary to document the omnipresence of this
rhetoric in deconstructionist writing. Suffice it to say that virtually
every sympathetic account of deconstruction at some point claims that
because deconstruction is so "infectious, corrosive, and irrepressible,"
it "regularly threatens all forms of convention" (I quote from Vincent
Leitch's recent *Deconstructive Criticism*).[4] It is this talk that has alarmed
so-called conservative critics of deconstruction, especially historical
scholars, who understandably see in such comments a massive repudi-
ation of their work. But these critics of deconstruction resemble irate
moviegoers who walk out on a film that is just getting started. After
giving deconstruction such power, Norris proceeds to strip away its
force, or at least to qualify its impact on the "traditional edifice" it
seems to topple. In his view, deconstruction is "not to be taken as
wholly undermining" the objects of its critique (48), whether Rousseau in the *Grammatology* or structuralism in "Structure, Sign, and
Play" (deconstruction is not "'post-structuralist' in the sense of dis-
placing or invalidating the structuralist project" [54]). More generally,

> Deconstruction neither denies nor really affects the commonsense view
> that language exists to communicate meaning. It *suspends* that view for
> its own specific purpose of seeing what happens when the writs of
> convention no longer run. . . . This is not to say that [the deconstruc-
> tionists'] questions are trivial or totally misconceived. They are . . .
> questions that present themselves *compulsively* as soon as one abandons
> the commonsense position. But language continues to communicate, as
> life goes on, despite all the problems thrown up by sceptical thought.
> (128)

Skeptics since David Hume, in short, have realized that "life could
scarcely carry on if people were to act on their conclusions" (xii);

deconstruction is "likewise an activity of thought which cannot be consistently acted on—that way madness lies—but which yet possesses an inescapable rigour of its own" (xii).

These are the disclaimers that have provoked many activist critics to conclude that deconstruction is therefore worthless, a fad that only a dwindling number of well-established professors have the luxury to enjoy. These opponents of deconstruction, however, seem to me as impatient as the conservative readers mentioned earlier. I take seriously Norris's further point that the deconstructionists' questions are neither "trivial" nor "totally misconceived." There is a potentially constructive side to deconstruction, to which I will return.

But first I should note that my own dissatisfaction begins with Norris's definition of "common sense" in the passages I have been citing. In my view, deconstruction offers liberation not from common sense but from extreme positions hardly anyone holds. As I have suggested repeatedly in this book, poststructuralists set up the admittedly vulnerable targets that they knock down when they argue that "the writer writes *in* a language and *in* a logic whose proper system, laws and life his discourse by definition cannot dominate absolutely" (Derrida); that the critic cannot "get his poet right in a final decisive formulation which will allow him to have done with that poet, once and for all" (Miller); and that "there is no divine or dialectical science that can help us purify history absolutely, to pass in our lifetime a last judgment on it" (Hartman).[5]

Norris betrays an analogous penchant for upending straw men when, commenting on Derrida's ascription of indeterminacy to writing, he notes that "the effect is unsettling not only for linguistics but for every field of enquiry based on the idea of an immediate, intuitive access to meaning" (30). I do not know of any field based on such an idea—linguistics included. In challenging the "idea of an immediate, intuitive access to meaning," Derrida is not overturning common sense but supporting it.

In much the same way, Norris notes that the "deconstructive leverage supplied by a term like *writing* depends on its resistance to any kind of settled or definitive meaning" (31). A Derridean term like "writing" or *différance,* in other words, "cannot be reduced to any single, self-identical meaning" (32). I do not know of any term that can be reduced to a single, invariable meaning: the meaning of every term (including "term") reflects the specific context in which the term occurs. The fact that the meaning of a word varies in this way shocks only those who "dream of a perfect, unimpeded communion of minds" (94). But for those who do not share this dream—and I would include most modern writers in this far from exclusive group— Derrida is smothering a hope that either never lived or died long ago.

Finally, borrowing an example from Roland Barthes to illustrate "the slippages of everyday referential meaning," Norris cites "the merest of telegraphic greetings: 'Monday. Returning tomorrow. Jean-Louis'" (112). Norris seems surprised that multiple ambiguities "lurk behind even such a simple and practical piece of language" (for example, *Which* Jean-Louis? *Which* of the various Mondays on which the message might have been penned?" [112]). I am surprised by Norris's astonishment: precisely because the message is so simple, because it is "the merest of telegraphic greetings," its meaning is unclear. The sparseness of the text invites the playful speculation that Norris finds so bold.

I have been suggesting that hardly anyone holds the ostensibly "traditional," "common-sense" positions that deconstruction assaults. More importantly, no one needs these positions to resist those conclusions that, in deconstruction, follow from the fact that we can never be absolutely sure about the meaning of a text. Deconstruction, again, argues that interpretation is not simply difficult but impossible: the meaning of Jean-Louis's telegram is a hole we can never fill. Derridean critics, in short, wake up from the "dream of a perfect, unimpeded communion of minds," only to find themselves cut off completely from the texts they thought they knew. As Norris puts it, commenting on Derrida's well-known contribution to *Deconstruction and Criticism,*

> The topic is ostensibly Shelley's poem 'The Triumph of Life', which serves as a focus for the other contributors but which barely manages to peep through the tangles and cunning indirections of Derrida's text. He makes no pretence of 'interpreting' the poem but uses its title and random associative hints as a springboard into regions of giddying uncertainty, where details merge and cross in a joyful breakdown of all proprietory limits. Any talk of meaning or structure is ineluctably 'caught up in a process which it does not control', which for Derrida signals the total dissolution of those boundaries that mark off one text

from another, or that try to interpose between poem and commentary.
(114)

Derrida does not choose to play with Shelley's poem; he has to play
with the poem, there being no objective "poem" or "meaning" for him
to know.

"Knowledge" here entails total control, and much of Norris's energy goes into showing that authors cannot constrain the interpretation of their texts. A text, to use terms that should by now be familiar,
"ramifies" or "disseminates" an author's intent, forcing readers to see
multiple possibilities and not a fixed "center" that governs the production of meaning. For Norris, following Derrida and de Man,
metaphors get the better of what an author tries to say. On virtually
every page, he speaks of "track[ing] down [a text] to its metaphors"
(119), of "combat[ing]" a text "by exposing its ruses of metaphor"
(88), of "tropes taking over the business of narrative or logical argument, substituting a play of figural language that obeys its own laws of
inverted cause-and-effect" (106). The "phraseology" of Marxist texts
in particular is "revealingly loose and metaphorical" (79) (for Norris
the two terms seem synonymous). Objecting to a passage from Terry
Eagleton's *Criticism and Ideology,* Norris complains that "the argument
here is entirely in the charge of its sustaining metaphors" (81); even
Eagleton's "elaborate argumentation cannot conceal its dependence
on these basic and proliferating figures of thought. . . . The Marxist
model of representation, however refined in theory, is caught up in a
rhetoric of tropes and images that entirely controls its logic" (83).

In pitting a text's metaphors against its claim to assert something
determinate and true, Norris is again employing a common tactic of
deconstruction. In his reading of Rousseau in *Of Grammatology,* Derrida establishes the precedent for Norris's procedure by locating the
opening for a deconstructive interpretation in the space between what
an author wishes to say or "declares" and what the tropes in his text
"describe." Instead of docilely ornamenting, adorning, or figuring
forth an author's meaning, metaphors, in this view, explode meaning,
once more demonstrating the force of language.

I agree with Norris and other deconstructionists that there is a logic
of metaphor. In some versions of Marxism, for instance, "base" generates "superstructure" and various mechanical ways of relating the two
terms. Sometimes, moreover, a metaphor can mislead an author. By

making it hard to picture the independent force of art, the base/superstructure metaphor has (mis)led some Marxists into supposing that art, like a superstructure, lacks influence on the economic base that ostensibly buttresses it. But because metaphors can control an argument, it hardly follows that they have to. Some texts resist the "seductions of metaphor" (103) that all texts face.

Take one of Norris's own metaphors: "thinking is always and inseparably bound to the rhetorical devices that support it" (61). E. D. Hirsch's critique of deconstruction to the contrary, a deconstructionist would concede that the intent of Norris's assertion is at first glance clear: thought collapses without metaphorical supports, much as a house is no longer a house when its foundation crumbles. Thinking, in other words, always takes place through metaphors.

But the very metaphors in Norris's statement (a deconstructionist reading might add) enforce the separation between tropes and thought that Norris wishes to repress. "Devices" and "supports," like the foundation of a house, preexist what they support. Norris's statement accordingly implies a sequence: metaphors come before the thoughts that are then inseparably bound to them. Metaphors, to be sure, constrain thinking (the way a foundation limits what can be built on it) but metaphors do not constitute thinking.

One can deconstruct Norris's statement this way, but I do not see any reason to take his comparison so literally (Norris shrewdly points out that Derrida's readings are "perverse but utterly literal" [33]. I would say, perverse because invariably literal). Norris's point in the statement I have been analyzing is that metaphors are like supports in some ways (i.e., without them, thought collapses), but unlike supports in other ways (i.e., metaphors are thoughts). One can read into Norris's tropes commitments that he does not endorse, but I find such an exercise gratuitous, inspired not by the text but by a dubious prior affirmation of the "bottomless relativity of meaning" (58). I can make this point, moreover, without falling back on the typically extreme position that Norris is attacking (here, the "repressive" claim that figurative language is only "a blemish on the surface of logical thought" [70]). One can grant that metaphors are powerful and even necessary without making them omnipotent.

In the view of metaphor that I am proposing here, metaphors are indispensable: we cannot weed them out of our writing, nor should we try. But although we cannot do without metaphors, we can nevertheless use them to make factual assertions. If metaphors are not optional tools or ornaments, neither are they sinister agents that always trap, combat, loosen, and finally take over the unsuspecting text that invites them in. Much more, of course, needs to be said about the uses (as well as the ruses) of metaphor.[6] Here, however, I want to suggest that by making metaphors omnipotent and thus hardening the indeterminacy of texts into a necessity, deconstructionists defuse their own enterprise—or admit to its lack of power—as shown by another glance at Jean-Louis's telegram, "Monday. Returning tomorrow. Jean-Louis."

According to Norris, we can "play with all the possible ambiguities that lurk behind even such a simple and practical piece of language," thereby defying "society," which "tries to bar such pleasurable vagaries by insisting on specific memoranda of dates, places, patronymics, and so forth" (112). While I agree that a society may try to limit the liberties we take with such a text, in my view conventions of interpretation may be enabling as well as constraining—more exactly, enabling because constraining, in the way, for instance, that tennis lessons, by curtailing our free play with the racket, permit us to hit the ball. (If I am anxious to pick up Jean-Louis at the airport, I may want to master the conventions that enable me to know what his telegram says.) But for Norris, conventions are only repressive: "all social existence," he says at one point, "is self-alienating" (40), inimical to the creative play that readers presumably always desire and all texts apparently encourage. In Norris's argument, the theoretical impossibility of extracting a determinate meaning from a text becomes an ominous practical necessity, backed up by force, never by desire. What we cannot do in theory—settle on a meaning—we unfortunately have to do in practice, to pass the course, stay clear of the police, and so forth.

My reference to the police recalls Derrida's comment, quoted earlier, that "the police is always waiting in the wings" to push an out-of-step reading into line. Because of the "fictionality that constitutes [conventions]," they are "by essence violable and precarious," requiring force to insure compliance with them. Elsewhere, Derrida suggests that these conventions are not "violable and precarious" but immensely powerful because they reside in language. Either way, whether supported by society or by language, these conventions are inescapable, some form of social organization being for Derrida as unavoidable as language. Following Derrida, revisionist critics routinely concede the immutability and necessity of what Norris calls "age-old conceptual limits," even as they claim to undermine their legitimacy. To cite only two examples of a central tendency in contemporary theory, although Hartman thinks that no form of closure should occur in interpretation (given the indeterminacy of literary texts), he admits that "forms of closure will occur," whether we want them to or not (given the demands of the institutions we must inhabit). Similarly, in a sweeping passage cited earlier, de Man observes at the conclusion of "Shelley Disfigured,"

> The Triumph of Life warns us that nothing, whether deed, word, thought or text, ever happens in relation, positive or negative, to anything that precedes, follows or exists elsewhere, but only as a random event whose power, like the power of death, is due to the randomness of its occurrence. It also warns us why and how these events then have to be reintegrated in a historical and aesthetic system of recuperation that repeats itself regardless of the exposure of its fallacy. (DC, 69)[7]

We have to continue "recuperating" and "monumentalizing" texts—that is, assigning them a shape and intention—even though we supposedly know that such an enterprise rests on a "fallacy" (here, the fallacy of attributing a design to random events). "No degree of knowledge," de Man continues, "can ever stop this madness, for it is the madness of words" (DC, 68).

Norris, like these other critics, concedes not only that there must be an authoritative, socially agreed upon reading of texts (or anarchy would result), but that this official reading must be arbitrary (given the radical undecidability of writing). It follows that either we placate authorities by acting as if their official interpretation is valid, or we play with texts as Barthes does, uncovering the possibilities that "society" suppresses. Instead of contradicting each other, these options occupy different moments in deconstruction. The first allows deconstructionists to get along in the world by humoring the consensus that by their own admission they cannot overturn; the second allows them to live with their powerlessness by letting them feel superior to the "common sense," "traditional" people who presumably believe in the official reading that deconstructionists see through. Out of convenience or necessity, deconstructionists may acquiesce to the established version of things—as Norris admits, "life could scarcely carry on if people were to act on their conclusions" (xii)—but they alone know that the public understanding of reality is a mere contrivance, in Norris's words, "nothing more than an empty or fallible convention" (111). Deconstructionists may be compliant, but at least they are not duped.

Jonathan Culler's *On Deconstruction* conveniently recapitulates the phases in deconstruction that I have been describing. First, Culler, like Norris, credits deconstruction with the power to "disrupt," "subvert," and "undo" numerous hierarchical distinctions, among them cause/effect, philosophy/literature, literal/figurative, man/woman, signified/signifier, understanding/misunderstanding, serious/nonserious, unity/heterogeneity, presence/absence, central/marginal, speech/writing, and referential/rhetorical. The distinction between cause and effect, for example, is "not an indubitable foundation but the product of a tropological operation" (87), a description that applies to the other dualisms that I have listed. All of them are "put in question"—or, what is the same thing to Culler, exposed as rhetorical strategies—by the very texts that rely on them for support.

Second, anxious to dissociate deconstruction from "an impetuous nihilism" (133) and to dispel "rumors that deconstructive criticism denigrates literature, celebrates the free associations of readers, and eliminates meaning and referentiality" (280), Culler, again like Norris, goes on to say that the distinctions cited above are "undone" but not "destroyed," "scrapped," or "abandoned." "The concept of causation," for instance, "is not an error that philosophy could or should have avoided but is indispensable—to the argument of deconstruction as to other arguments" (87). Similarly, deconstructing the signified/signifier opposition does "not mean that the notion of sign could or should be scrapped; on the contrary, the distinction between what signifies and what is signified is essential to any thought whatever" (188). Other "subverted" dualisms are also retained, such as unity/heterogeneity ("deconstruction leads not to a brave new world in which unity never figures but to the identification of unity as a problematical figure" [200]) and literal/figurative, a distinction "essential to discussions of the functioning of language" (150). Culler's own study of deconstruction illustrates the retention of such allegedly undone notions as "making clear," "grasping," "demonstrating," "revealing," and "showing what is the case," all of which "invoke presence" (94) and all of which figure prominently in a book that hopes "to contend with bafflement" (17) and "to dispel confusion" (18).[8]

Third, despite the persistence of the categories that deconstruction ostensibly subverts, Culler still wants to praise its "significant effects" (176) and the "changes" it has wrought (or will bring about) in "assumptions, institutions, and practices" (154), changes that make it one of the "most vital and significant" developments in recent theory. Deconstructing a distinction, while not destroying or invalidating it, nonetheless "gives it a different status and impact": an undone distinction "works differently" and "does not have the same implications" (150). Pursuing these "changes" and "implications," however, is like trying to pin down a mirage, as Culler continually defers the precise account of these changes that he leads us to expect. At the outset he warns us that these consequences of deconstruction "have not proved easy to calculate" (156), then he cautions that they "may be slow to work themselves out" (157), and finally he concedes that they may not come about at all:

> The implications of deconstruction for literary study must be inferred, but it is not clear how such inferences are to be made. The argument that all readings are misreadings, for example, does not seem to have logical consequences that would compel critics to proceed differently, yet it may well affect the way critics think about reading and the questions they pose about acts of interpretation. In this case as in others, that is to say, the deconstruction of a hierarchical opposition does not entail or compel changes in literary criticism, yet it can have considerable impact on how critics proceed. (180)

It "*can* have considerable impact," in other words, but it does not have to, there being nothing in the theory that mandates the changes that Culler initially promises deconstruction will bring.

In my view, Culler's account of the significant changes wrought by deconstruction does not get anywhere because it has nowhere to go. As I have been suggesting, deconstruction in practice remains trapped in the conventions that theoretically it claims to dissolve. The upshot of deconstruction is not qualitative change but more of the same, not revolution but repetition, or, as Culler himself puts it, not "skeptical detachment" but "unwarrantable involvement" in structures that it cannot justify (88). Instead of advancing, deconstruction is floundering, mired in the very system that it calls groundless.

Constantly in motion, verbally assaulting all social conventions, deconstruction nevertheless goes nowhere—like running in place. Its place, I have been arguing, is the university, where most of its adherents work. Instead of threatening the university and, by extension, the larger society with which the university interacts, deconstruction leaves existing institutions more secure, as a brief look at my second example, J. Hillis Miller's "The Function of Rhetorical Study at the Present Time," shows.

In part, Miller's essay is a perceptive, if by now familiar, comment on the plight of literary studies: put simply, the students taking literature courses in steadily declining numbers are understandably less prepared and less motivated than their predecessors. In Miller's opinion, we can take several steps to improve things. First, we should integrate the study of literature with our burgeoning programs in expository writing: "Learning to write well cannot be separated from learning to read well."[9] Second, we should reexamine our largely chronological "periodization" of literary history and the curriculum, considering more fluid models, like Harold Bloom's family romance or the dialectical scheme of Marxism: "By what right, according to what measure, guided or supported by what reason, is this framing [of historical periods] performed? What justifies it, as one justifies a line of type, rules it, and keeps it from straggling all down the page? Is periodization a free positing or the referential recording of a knowledge?" (14). Third, we should ask the same questions of the boundaries we have drawn around genres, even around imaginative writing itself.

Deconstruction ("rhetorical study" in Miller's title) motivates these questions. Like Norris, Miller tracks down texts to their metaphors, in this case the figures of speech that organize the curriculum (metonymy, for example, when the name of a monarch stands for an entire period, as in "Edwardian" or "Victorian," metaphor when a stylistic feature assimilates the period to nature, making a period seem "rough, like an irregular pearl," in the case of the "baroque," or "self-born, born anew," in the case of "the Renaissance"). The figurative status of these categories prompts Miller to suspect their necessity: "Does the name of a period indicate its intrinsic essence, its very being, or is it a convenient fiction? . . . The question is whether the chosen part is genuinely similar to the whole, metaphorically valid, or whether it is a mere contingent metonymy, a piece of a heterogeneous mixture chosen arbitrarily to stand for the whole or to make a melange without intrinsic unity seem like a whole" (15).

Lest Miller's concern for the curriculum and other educational matters seem an exception to what prevails elsewhere in deconstructionist theory, I should note that numerous constructive ideas are struggling to be born in the criticism that I have been attacking. Like Miller, Stanley Fish, for example, suggests that if literature is an "open category" defined by "what we decide to put in it," not by inherent qualities such as ambiguity or a disregard for propositional truth, then we should investigate the cultural presuppositions that shape our reading of literary works. Culler astutely points out the educational importance of this question: "We often complain that students have not read enough when they come to college, but the problem is not a quantitative one that would be solved by more assigned readings. The problem is structural, involving the marginal situation of literature within the students' cultures." That is, the problem is not simply that students have not read enough but that they do not know how to read. Because "literature is simply one aspect of their culture, and an aspect with which they are relatively unfamiliar," they have not assimilated the interpretive conventions that enable texts to have meaning. Culler proposes courses (on narrative, for example) that would examine literature along with other kinds of writing, enabling us to teach the requisite interpretive procedures and to show that literary works are not only "monuments of a specialized high culture" but "powerful, elegant, self-conscious, or perhaps self-indulgent manifestations of common patterns of sense-making."[10]

Finally, deploring "the lack of interaction between [the literary humanities] and the mainstream of society" (*CW,* 284), the gap between advanced studies and everyday classroom teaching, our inability to "formulate an effective defense of our profession" (*CW,* 292), and the consequent "impotence" of literary study, Hartman proposes carrying the "concept of liberal education . . . upward, into the graduate and professional schools" (*CW,* 294). To "encourage contact between the professions,"

> medical students should be asked to take an advanced course in literary (or art) interpretation; so should students of law. . . . A single course may seem like a palliative. Very well: can we devise joint programs without jeopardizing the standing of the candidate? Is it so unthinkable to have a degree in English and in Law, Religious Studies, or Business? Could the universities, with the help of the foundations, establish continuing-education supplements in these fields? (*CW,* 294)

Conversely, students of literature should be exposed "not only to literature narrowly conceived but also to important texts in philosophy, history, religion, anthropology, and so forth" (*CW*, 296). "Unless we find some doors, revolving or not, that lead from the humanities into society," Hartman warns, "and unless some of our graduates go into other walks of life than teaching, or remain in touch with us even though they are in the nonacademic professions, the humanities are bound to become service departments to other divisions of the academy with more obvious and effective social outlets" (*CW*, 288).

Hartman's proposals, like Miller's and Culler's, are promising, but a skeptical theory of meaning takes the ground out from under them—or never gives them ground on which to stand. I have already shown why Hartman's commitment to the terminal elusiveness of literary meaning, far from remedying the "impotence" of literary study, exacerbates it. Similarly, in Miller's case, deconstruction nullifies the skepticism it inspires, making the questions Miller asks of historical periods, genres, and literature disingenuous. Despite his holding out the possibility of "valid" categories, he knows in advance—he always already knows—that all conceptions of literary history are merely convenient fictions, invented, in his words, for " 'political purposes,' according to one or another mode of figurative reduction," imposing coherence on the inaccessible facts (15). This knowledge (that all historical categories are "baseless" figures of speech) is somehow "not itself period-bound" but "part of any period in our history" (14). Miller notes that "the traditional historical organization by periods and genres should be dismantled only when we are sure we have alternatives that will be better" (17). But if all historical frameworks are as illegitimate as the "traditional historical" one, then it would seem best to leave things as they are. To the question, "Who has the right to name the period?" Miller answers, No one—or anyone. Any scheme for improvement is as groundless as the model it would replace.

A proposal that starts out promising change thus ends up discouraging it. Miller's analysis of the novel applies to his own deconstruction of the curriculum: "It is a throwing away of what is already thrown away in order to save it. It is a destroying of the already destroyed, in order to preserve the illusion that it is still intact" (16–17). Many of us suspect that the present historical organization of our subject matter is, in Miller's words, a "vast shifting fabrication." But after articulating this suspicion, Miller undermines it by concluding that all schemes suffer from the groundlessness that vitiates the present one.

As the texts I have been examining suggest, deconstruction does make a difference: it reinforces established political and educational arrangements rather than damaging them or leaving them as they are. Seeming to light out for new territory, deconstruction stays at home in the profession that it disdains. The often noted assimilation of deconstruction by the university thus does not indicate the tolerance or self-destructiveness of the university but the docility of deconstruction. Instead of challenging what Norris calls the "solemn conventions of Anglo-American academic discourse" (113), deconstruction allows us to live with them.

NOTES

I: Matthew Arnold and Contemporary Criticism

All references to Matthew Arnold's works are to *The Complete Prose Works of Matthew Arnold,* ed. R. H. Super (Ann Arbor: University of Michigan Press, 1960–77), 11 vols. I cite *Culture and Anarchy* (Volume 5) as *CA.*

1. Northrop Frye, *Anatomy of Criticism* (Princeton: Princeton University Press, 1957), p. 18.

2. Geoffrey Hartman, *Criticism in the Wilderness* (New Haven: Yale University Press, 1980), pp. 174, 253. Cited in text as *CW.*

3. Eugene Goodheart, "Arnold at the Present Time," *Critical Inquiry* 9 (March 1983): 460, 468.

4. Morris Dickstein, "Arnold Then and Now: The Use and Misuse of Criticism," *Critical Inquiry* 9 (March 1983): 497.

5. Along similar lines, in "Matthew Arnold: The Artist in the Wilderness," *Critical Inquiry* 9 (March 1983): 469–82, George Levine has argued that Arnold is "very much alive in the criticism [he] is so often invoked to combat," in part because his critical practice is at odds with his theory. We can neither "claim Arnold as a spiritual father to a newer criticism with a deep social purpose and strong connections with history and society"—as Goodheart and Dickstein want to do—nor use him "to demonstrate the dangers of a criticism weakly submitting itself to the authority of a text and accepting its own, unimaginative marginality," as Hartman does in *Criticism in the Wilderness* (477). I reach a comparable conclusion, though instead of arguing that Arnold's practice belies his ideals, I try to show that his theory is at odds with itself.

6. Frederic Harrison, "Our Venetian Constitution," *Fortnightly Review* 7 (March 1867): 276–77. Quoted by Arnold in *Culture and Anarchy,* pp. 87–88.

7. John Ruskin, *The Stones of Venice,* in *The Genius of John Ruskin,* ed. John D. Rosenberg (Boston: Houghton Mifflin, 1963), pp. 180, 177, 182.

8. H. L. Lowry, ed., *The Letters of Matthew Arnold to Arthur Hugh Clough* (New York: Oxford University Press, 1932), p. 146.

9. Lowry, pp. 63, 66.

10. Many critics have noted that Arnold's reluctance to claim objective truth for poetry distinguishes him from his romantic predecessors. See especially William A. Madden, *Matthew Arnold: A Study of the Aesthetic Temperament in Victorian England* (Bloomington: Indiana University Press, 1967), p. 194; Leon Gottfried, *Matthew Arnold and the Romantics* (Lincoln: University of Nebraska Press, 1963), pp. 200–18; and Murray Krieger, "The Critical Legacy of Matthew Arnold; Or, The Strange Brotherhood of T. S. Eliot, I. A. Richards and Northrop Frye," *The Southern Review* 5 (1969): 457–74.

11. Lionel Trilling, *Matthew Arnold* (1938; rpt. New York: Meridian Books, 1955), pp. 323, 333. Pseudostatement is, of course, I. A. Richards's term for assertions in poems that have the form, but not the function, of propositions.

The criticisms I make here of Arnold also apply to Richards, who often acknowledged his indebtedness to Arnold. On the problems Arnold encountered in claiming a social function for poetry, see also Vincent Buckley, *Poetry and Morality* (London: Chatto and Windus, 1968), pp. 45–76.

12. J. M. Wilson, "On Teaching Natural Sciences in Schools," in *Essays on a Liberal Education*, ed. F. W. Farrar (London: Macmillan, 1867), p. 251. For further evidence of the identification of scientific experiment with rational knowledge, see Thomas H. Huxley, *Science and Education* (New York: D. Appleton, 1896) and Alfred W. Benn, *History of English Rationalism in the Nineteenth Century* (1906; rpt. New York: Russell and Russell, 1962).

13. As an apologist for Christianity, T. S. Eliot made much the same point. Although the early Eliot did not object to Arnold's assigning an emotional rather than intellectual function to poetry, he saw that such a limitation made poetry a "superior amusement," not a criticism of life, antidote to anarchy, or substitute for religion. Especially not the latter: after his conversion to Christianity, Eliot argued that detaching the values of Christianity from the beliefs that once occasioned them is like expecting support from the wallpaper after the wall has crumbled. See his "Literature, Science, and Dogma," *The Dial* 82 (March 1927): 243. However, Eliot's attempt to rehabilitate the truth of religion did not entail a comparable effort on behalf of the truth of poetry.

14. J. D. Jump, *Matthew Arnold* (London: Longmans, Green, & Co., 1955), p. 67. On Arnold's needs and circumstances, see also J. Hillis Miller, *The Disappearance of God* (Cambridge: Harvard University Press, 1963), pp. 241–69, and E. D. H. Johnson, *The Alien Vision of Victorian Poetry* (1952; rpt. Hamden: Archon Books, 1963), pp. 152–217.

15. Quoted in J. W. Saunders, *The Profession of English Letters* (London: Routledge and Kegan Paul, 1964), p. 204. William Morris also linked the health of culture to equality:

> I do not believe in the possibility of keeping art vigorously alive by the action, however energetic, of a few groups of specially gifted men and their small circle of admirers amidst a general public incapable of understanding and enjoying their work. I hold firmly to the opinion that all worthy schools of art must be in the future, as they have been in the past, the outcome of the aspirations of the people towards the beauty and true pleasure of life. . . . These aspirations of the people towards beauty can only be born from a condition of practical equality. . . .

November 10, 1893 letter quoted in E. P. Thompson, *William Morris* (New York: Pantheon Books, 1976), pp. 664–65. In an 1884 speech on preservation Morris made the same point more vividly:

> Believe me, it will not be possible for a small knot of cultivated people to keep alive an interest in the art and records of the past amidst the present conditions of a sordid and heart-breaking struggle for existence for the many, and a languid sauntering through life for the few. But when society is so reconstituted that all citizens will have a chance made up of due leisure and reasonable work, then will all society . . . resolve to protect ancient buildings . . .

(Quoted in Thompson, p. 241).

16. For a sharp discussion of the shortcomings of Arnold's politics, especially of his unwavering commitment to middle-class rule, see Raymond Wil-

liams, *Culture and Society 1780–1950* (1958; rpt. New York: Harper and Row, 1966), pp. 110–29.

17. The radical critics I have in mind here are several of the contributors to *The Politics of Literature,* a collection of "dissenting essays on the teaching of English," ed. Louis Kampf and Paul Lauter (New York: Random House, 1972).

II: The Imagination as a Sanction of Value

1. Northrop Frye, *Spiritus Mundi* (Bloomington: Indiana University Press, 1976), p. 14.

2. Northrop Frye, *The Stubborn Structure* (Ithaca: Cornell University Press, 1970), p. 160.

3. Northrop Frye, *A Study of English Romanticism* (New York: Random House, 1968), p. 14.

4. Frye, *The Stubborn Structure,* p. 172.

5. See Cleanth Brooks, *The Well Wrought Urn* (New York: Harvest Books, 1947), pp. 202, 252, 264, 266.

6. See also Gerald Graff, *Poetic Statement and Critical Dogma* (Evanston: Northwestern University Press, 1970): "The root of the problem is that the desire of post-Ricardian New Critics to claim an objective knowledge for poetry conflicts with assumptions that preclude the very possibility of objective knowledge. If the formulations of reason have no relevance to the deeper realities of experience, and if poetry is not predicated on rational knowledge, then it is not clear on what grounds objective truth can be claimed" (16).

7. Northrop Frye, *The Educated Imagination* (Bloomington: Indiana University Press, 1964), pp. 80–81.

8. Frye, *The Stubborn Structure,* p. 51.

9. Ibid., p. 54.

10. Northrop Frye, *Fables of Identity* (New York: Harcourt, Brace & World, 1963), p. 151.

11. Northrop Frye, *The Secular Scripture* (Cambridge: Harvard University Press, 1976), p. 46.

12. Northrop Frye, *Creation and Recreation* (Toronto: University of Toronto Press, 1980), pp. 7, 8, 9.

13. Oscar Wilde, *Intentions,* in *The Artist as Critic,* ed. Richard Ellmann (New York: Vintage Books, 1970), p. 330.

14. Frye, *Anatomy of Criticism,* pp. 347–48. To critics (and admirers) who assert that he neglects "the social reference of literary criticism," Frye replies, "I have written about practically nothing else" (*The Stubborn Structure,* p. x).

15. Northrop Frye, *The Modern Century* (Toronto: Oxford University Press, 1967), p. 45.

16. Frye, *Creation and Recreation,* pp. 17, 18–19.

17. Frye, *Anatomy of Criticism,* p. 347.

18. Northrop Frye, *Fearful Symmetry* (1947; rpt. Princeton: Princeton University Press, 1969), p. 90.

19. Frye, *The Stubborn Structure,* p. 198. As Frye makes this point in *The Modern Century,* art liberates our imagination rather than provides us with "a statement both of what is believed to be true and of what is going to be true by a course of action" (p. 116). Our imagination frees us, but "all forms of

politics, including the radical form, seem sooner or later to dwindle into a specialized chess game" (p. 101).

20. Northrop Frye, *The Critical Path* (Bloomington: Indiana University Press, 1971), p. 133.

21. Frye, *The Secular Scripture*, p. 173. Frye illustrates this point by appealing to romance in romantic literature (see *A Study of English Romanticism*, pp. 37–40) and to Shakespeare's later plays (see *Fools of Time* [Toronto: University of Toronto Press, 1967], pp. 120–21, and *A Natural Perspective* [New York: Harcourt, Brace & World, 1965], pp. 75–117).

22. Frye, *The Stubborn Structure*, p. 256, and "Presidential Address 1976," *PMLA* 92 (May 1977): 389.

23. Frye, *The Critical Path*, p. 170.

24. Frye, "Presidential Address 1976," 388. Richard Kostelanetz's excellent profile of Frye—"The Literature Professor's Literature Professor," *The Michigan Quarterly Review* 17 (Fall 1978): 425–42—shows that the humanity that distinguishes Frye's writing also informs his relationships with his students and colleagues. "With evident pain" he tells Kostelanetz of a department meeting the preceding day, when three junior professors had come up for tenure: "The demands made on young academics today, in order to grant them tenure, are so great that, if I were thirty years old today, I'd question going into academic work. I'd head for the Civil Service, where the requirements have a more human scale" (434).

25. Frye, *The Critical Path*, pp. 104–105.

26. Gerald Graff, *Literature Against Itself* (Chicago: University of Chicago Press, 1979), pp. 188–89.

27. See, for example, Henry B. Veatch, *For an Ontology of Morals* (Evanston: Northwestern University Press, 1971), a defense of grounding moral distinctions in human nature. See also Wayne C. Booth's attempt to reconnect "passionate commitment" with "good reasons" in *Now Don't Try to Reason with Me* (Chicago: University of Chicago Press, 1970) and *Modern Dogma and the Rhetoric of Assent* (Chicago: University of Chicago Press, 1974). The latter provides an excellent bibliography of recent efforts to derive what ought to be from what is.

28. See Blake's *A Vision of the Last Judgment*, in *The Poetry and Prose of William Blake*, ed. David V. Erdman (Garden City: Doubleday, 1970), pp. 555, 544, and *All Religions are One*, p. 2.

29. See my "Marxism and English Romanticism: The Persistence of the Romantic Movement," *Romanticism Past and Present* 6 (1982): 27–46.

30. Frye, *The Critical Path*, p. 119.

31. In "The Construal of Reality: Criticism in Modern and Postmodern Science," *Critical Inquiry* 9 (September 1982), Stephen Toulmin picks up where I leave off here. Toulmin first shows that "the mere presence . . . of an interpretive element in the natural sciences does nothing to detract from the objectivity of scientific results" (100). He then argues that the same is true of the humanities: the interpretive or concerned status of literary discourse need not annul its cognitive claims. Frye, I have been suggesting, endorses Toulmin's first point but inexplicably stops short of his second point—at great cost to his defense of literature. Toulmin concludes that "critical judgment in the natural sciences . . . is not geometrical" (in Frye's terms, even detached writing is concerned) "and critical interpretation in the humanities is not

whimsical" (concerned writing can still be detached). "In both spheres, the proper aims should be the same—that is, to be perceptive, illuminating, and reasonable" (111).

32. Frank Kermode, *The Sense of an Ending* (New York: Oxford University Press, 1967), p. 58.

33. Ibid., p. 41.

34. Ibid., p. 13.

35. Similarly, when I go on to say that Arnold resists deconstruction, I use "deconstruction" in a theoretical rather than a historical sense. By "deconstruction" I mean here not *Of Grammatology* (which Arnold, of course, never read) but a set of assumptions that recent critics have contrasted to Arnold's critical ideas.

36. Frye, *Creation and Recreation*, p. 53. In *Northrop Frye and Critical Method* (University Park: Pennsylvania State University Press, 1978), R. D. Denham ably defends Frye against the charge that he neglects the relationship of literature to life. But, anxious to show that Frye does not ignore values, Denham leaves unexplored the consequence of Frye's turning them into myths of concern. See also Denham's introduction to *Northrop Frye on Culture and Literature*, ed. Robert D. Denham (Chicago: University of Chicago Press, 1978), pp. 4, 10. For a fuller discussion of Denham's book, see my review in *Clio* 9 (Winter 1980): 478–80.

III: Poststructuralist Critical Theory

1. I paraphrase here a remark by Christopher Lasch in "Recovering Reality," *Salmagundi* 42 (Summer–Fall 1978): "Those positions that seem most radical—most uncompromising in their opposition to bourgeois cultural hegemony—often turn out today to render the most effective reinforcement to the status quo. . . . [T]he problem goes deeper than our society's well-known capacity to absorb dangerous ideas. The ideas associated with the politics of 'cultural revolution' have in fact ceased to be dangerous" (44). The fullest account of the harmony between deconstruction and contemporary American society is Graff's *Literature Against Itself*, an indispensable book for anyone interested in recent criticism.

2. Jacques Derrida, *Writing and Difference*, trans. Alan Bass (Chicago: University of Chicago Press, 1978), p. 9.

3. Ibid., p. 292.

4. See Derrida's reading of Rousseau in *Of Grammatology*, trans. Gayatri Chakravorty Spivak (Baltimore: The Johns Hopkins University Press, 1976), especially pp. 141–64. J. Hillis Miller deconstructs Booth's assertion—more precisely, M. H. Abrams's citation of Booth's comment—in "The Critic as Host," in Harold Bloom et al., *Deconstruction and Criticism* (New York: Seabury Press, 1979), pp. 217–53. Cited in text as *DC*.

5. Derrida, *Writing and Difference*, p. 64.

6. Ibid., p. 263.

7. In "Stevens' Rock and Criticism as Cure, II," *The Georgia Review* 30 (Summer 1976), J. Hillis Miller describes the disorientation that results:

In a different way in each case, the work of the uncanny critics, however reasonable or sane their apparent procedure, reaches a point where it resists the intelligence almost successfully. At this point it no longer quite makes rational sense, and the reader has the uncomfortable feeling that he cannot quite hold

what is being said in his mind or make it all fit. Sooner or later there is the
encounter with an "aporia" or impasse. The bottom drops out, or there is an
"abyssing," an insight one can almost grasp or recognize as part of the familiar
landscape of the mind, but not quite, as though the mental eye could not quite
bring the material into lucid focus. (337–38)

8. For further discussion of this conservative streak in deconstruction, see
Gerald Graff, "Deconstruction as Dogma, or 'Come Back to the Raft Ag'in,
Strether Honey,'" *The Georgia Review* 34 (Summer 1980): 407. In addition to
Graff, other critics have noticed dogmatic, even authoritarian tendencies in
deconstruction. See especially Frank Lentricchia's discussion of Paul de Man's
"rhetoric of authority" in *After the New Criticism* (Chicago: University of
Chicago Press, 1980), pp. 282–317; William E. Cain, "Deconstruction in
America: The Recent Literary Criticism of J. Hillis Miller," *College English* 41
(December 1979): 367–82 ("Deconstruction," Cain shows, "argues *against*
privilege, but must privilege its own insights"); and David J. Gordon, "The
Story of a Critical Idea," *Partisan Review* 47 (1980): 107–108.

9. Jacques Derrida, "Signature Event Context," *Glyph 1* (Baltimore: The
Johns Hopkins University Press, 1977), p. 182. Cited in text as "SEC."

10. Jacques Derrida, "Limited Inc abc . . . ," *Glyph 2* (Baltimore: The Johns
Hopkins University Press, 1977), p. 250. Cited in text as "LI."

11. Derrida, *Of Grammatology*, p. 158.

12. Ibid.

13. See "Signature Event Context," p. 172. For a compelling critique of
Derrida's all-or-nothing attitudes, see Graff, "Deconstruction as Dogma," pp.
418–19; M. H. Abrams, "How to Do Things with Texts," *Partisan Review* 46
(1979): 570–75; and Charles Altieri, *Act and Quality* (Amherst: University of
Massachusetts Press, 1981), pp. 26–39, 225–29.

14. E. D. Hirsch accordingly accuses Derrida and other "cognitive atheists"
of ethical inconsistency. See *The Aims of Interpretation* (Chicago: University of
Chicago Press, 1967), pp. 13, 91. See also M. H. Abrams's similar comment on
J. Hillis Miller in "The Deconstructive Angel," *Critical Inquiry* 3 (Spring 1977):
436–38.

15. Harold Bloom, *The Anxiety of Influence* (New York: Oxford University
Press, 1973), p. 13.

16. Stanley Fish, *Is There a Text in This Class?* (Cambridge: Harvard Univer-
sity Press, 1980), p. 360. Cited in text as *TC*. For comparable institutional
accounts of interpretation, see John M. Ellis, *The Theory of Literary Criticism*
(Berkeley: University of California Press, 1974); Jonathan Culler, *Structuralist
Poetics* (Ithaca: Cornell University Press, 1975), especially chapter 6, "Literary
Competence"; and several recent works by Frank Kermode, including *The
Genesis of Secrecy* (Cambridge: Harvard University Press, 1979), "Institutional
Control of Interpretation," *Salmagundi* 43 (Winter 1979): 72–86, and "Can
We Say Absolutely Anything We Like?" in *Art, Politics, and Will,* ed. Quentin
Anderson et al. (New York: Basic Books, 1977), pp. 159–72. On Ellis, see
John Reichert, *Making Sense of Literature* (Chicago: University of Chicago
Press, 1977), pp. 150–55. On Culler, see Altieri, *Act and Quality*, pp. 184ff. On
Kermode, see my "Criticism, Inc.," *Salmagundi* 50–51 (Fall 1980–Winter
1981): 309–14.

17. Stanley E. Fish, "With the Compliments of the Author: Reflections on
Austin and Derrida," *Critical Inquiry* 8 (Summer 1982): 693–721. Fish notes
that his effort in this article "may appear to be simply one more American

domestication of Derridean thought, but it is intended as a counterweight to the more familiar domestication associated with words like 'undecidability' and the 'abyss' " (693).

18. In addition to the problem posed by my aligning Fish with Derrida, Fish's extraordinary intellectual mobility raises the problem of discussing his work at all. Unfortunately for anyone trying to refute him, he changes positions fast: rumor has it that he has recently repudiated, or veered away from, the ideas that I attribute to him in this chapter. (He has presumably developed a way of arguing of the superiority of some interpretive communities over others.) I can hardly respond to an argument that I have not seen (and which may not exist), but I mention this problem because it points up a common desire of poststructuralist writers—the desire to escape criticism. Cryptic writers like Derrida and Hartman evade criticism by stating their views so obliquely that they seem always able to say that their opponent (Searle, for instance) has misrepresented them. Fish cannot resort to this tactic: he writes much too clearly. Instead of refusing to be clear, he refuses to stand still. He not only disowns his earlier views but makes his critics seem humorless for taking them seriously ("Not to worry," is his genial advice). The agility of these writers, whether achieved by obfuscating their positions or by shifting them, makes their views not only frustrating to argue with but also difficult to defend. Taken to an extreme, such evasiveness exempts these writers from criticism but only by making it hard to say anything about their work. Praise becomes as problematic as refutation.

19. Ralph W. Rader, "Fact, Theory, and Literary Explanation," *Critical Inquiry* 1 (December 1974): 246–47. I agree with Rader, however, when he goes on to assert that there is a "cognitive basis for the agreement" of critics, "a basis in principle universally apprehensible and implying the common competence of the author and the collective and individual reader" (249). When we test some collective judgments, we find that "the integrity of our personal experience . . . is not coerced or distorted by the pressure of collective experience, the whims of anthropologists, or the quirks of tradition; we find rather that our experience has been anticipated by the collective experience and is surprisingly able to replicate it and, in the face of conflict, even to correct its own defects, as witness the sophomore who comes to love Pope" (248).

20. Despite their other differences, for both Fish and Derrida some form of coercion must finally determine interpretive decisions. For an astute discussion of this side of Derrida, see Lentricchia, *After the New Criticism*, pp. 174–77.

21. Ellis, *The Theory of Literary Criticism*, pp. 37–42. At one point Ellis notes that "weeds are a matter of hard empirical fact in our lives: they are indeed tangible and have distinct physical qualities that cause problems for us" (39). It seems to me that such a term describes the world as well as organizes it.

22. In *Is There a Text in This Class?*, Fish anticipates this objection (pp. 358–59) but does not answer it, for reasons I discuss on pp. 45–47.

23. John Reichert, "Making Sense of Interpretation," *Critical Inquiry* 6 (Summer 1980): 748. In "The Avoidance of Love: A Reading of *King Lear*," Stanley Cavell, attacking the problem of meaning from a different direction, sums up the point I have been trying to make in this discussion of Derrida and Fish: "Because the connection between using a word and meaning what it says is not inevitable or automatic, one may wish to call it a matter of convention. But then one must not suppose that it is a convention we would know how to forgo [or, I would add, that we should want to forgo]. It is not a matter

of convenience or ritual, unless having language is a convenience or unless thinking and speaking are rituals." *Must We Mean What We Say?* (1969; rpt. Cambridge: Cambridge University Press, 1976), pp. 270–71.

24. The references in this paragraph are to J. Hillis Miller, "Deconstructing the Deconstructers," *Diacritics* 5 (Summer 1975): 26, 30, 27. For a less sympathetic critique of Riddel, see Michael F. Harper, "Truth and Calliope: Ezra Pound's Malatesta," *PMLA* 96 (January 1981): 86–103, an excellent reply to Riddel's Derridean interpretation of *The Cantos* as a "signifying machine."

25. In "Deconstruction in America: The Recent Literary Criticism of J. Hillis Miller," William E. Cain notes that Miller's criticism depends on two unreconcilable ideas of the self. The first, a product of his early work under the influence of Georges Poulet, grants the self such powers as creation, self-consciousness, and choice. The second, a result of his new commitment to deconstruction, writes off the self as yet another linguistic construction. Miller's inability to reconcile these ideas comes out clearly in his well-known articles on Georges Poulet, cited by Cain on p. 369.

26. Commenting on Miller's "Ariachne's Broken Woof," *The Georgia Review* 31 (1977): 44–63, Charles Altieri notes, "One important reason why Miller grants no privileged model for holistically constructing a text is his absolute standard for deciding whether a context is appropriate or not: 'How can one stop the widening circle of contextual echoes with a difference,' if context 'can nowhere be fully identified or fully controlled'" (pp. 58–59). As in Derrida, Altieri observes, "absolutist terms like *fully* only betray an unwillingness to grant any probabilistic criteria. This refusal demands a great deal of theoretical justification it has not yet received." *Act and Quality*, p. 141, n. 31.

27. I take this phrase from Miller's analysis of *The Elective Affinities*, still "another demonstration of the self-subverting heterogeneity of each great work of Western literature." "This heterogeneity," Miller continues, broadening his claims even further, "of our great literary texts is one important manifestation of the equivocity of the Western tradition generally." Still further, "this equivocity is present in the languages we have to express ourselves in that tradition, and in the lives we have led in terms of those languages." "A 'Buchstäbliches' Reading of *The Elective Affinities*," *Glyph 6* (Baltimore: The Johns Hopkins University Press, 1979), p. 11.

28. Ibid., p. 23.

29. J. Hillis Miller, *Fiction and Repetition* (Cambridge: Harvard University Press, 1982), p. 3. Cited in text as *FR*.

IV: Revisionist Criticism in Practice

1. Tilottama Rajan, *Dark Interpreter: The Discourse of Romanticism* (Ithaca: Cornell University Press, 1980), p. 58, n. 2. Subsequent references are inserted in the text.

2. M. H. Abrams, *Natural Supernaturalism* (New York: W. W. Norton, 1971), p. 441. For a deconstructive critique of *Natural Supernaturalism* comparable to Rajan's, see J. Hillis Miller, "Tradition and Difference," *Diacritics* 1 (Winter 1972): 6–13.

3. Abrams, *Natural Supernaturalism*, p. 441.

4. Ibid., pp. 446, 462.

5. Harold Bloom, *Poetry and Repression* (New Haven: Yale University Press, 1976), p. 104. Subsequent references are inserted in the text.

6. Carlos Baker, *Shelley's Major Poetry: The Fabric of Vision* (Princeton: Princeton University Press, 1948), p. 257.

7. Ibid., p. 264.

8. A part of Shelley probably does reject Wordsworth's ideas because they are Wordsworth's. Bloom errs when he suggests that in the romantic period self-interest displaces rather than accompanies other reasons for writing. For a critique of Bloom comparable to my own, see Denis Donoghue, *Ferocious Alphabets* (Boston: Little, Brown, 1981), p. 145.

9. I take these phrases from *Prometheus Unbound:*

> If the abyss
> Could vomit forth its secrets.—But a voice
> Is wanting, the deep truth is imageless.
>
> (II.iv.114–16)

"Hymn to Intellectual Beauty" makes much the same point:

> No voice from some sublimer world hath ever
> To sage or poet these responses given—
> Therefore the names of Demon, Ghost, and Heaven,
> Remain the records of their vain endeavour,
> Frail spells. . . .
>
> (ll. 25–29)

10. *A Defence of Poetry,* in *Shelley's Critical Prose,* ed. Bruce R. McElderry, Jr. (Lincoln: University of Nebraska Press, 1967), p. 8.

11. Ibid., p. 6.

12. Abrams, though, does acknowledge "two voices" in Shelley, one a "public, vatic voice," the other a "private voice" that "does not sustain the assurance of the prophet, but expresses sharp oscillations of mood. . . ." "At times," Abrams adds, "exhausted by rejection, isolation, failure to reach an audience, and the repeated blows of private disasters, [Shelley] exhibits himself as more than half in love with easeful death" (*Natural Supernaturalism,* pp. 439–40). Abrams also allows for valid readings of romanticism other than his own, including one that would focus on romantic irony and make Byron its central figure. See his "Imagination and Rationality in Cultural History," *Critical Inquiry* 2 (Spring 1976): 447–64.

13. Although I cannot document the point here, Shelley's wavering seems to me typically romantic. Rajan is right to say that "critics such as Abrams and Earl Wasserman . . . take into account the darker side of Romanticism, but do not always recognize how far these elements threaten traditional Romantic postulates" (19). She successfully shows that romanticism, and not only Shelley, anticipates the "ambivalences of Modernism" (260, n. 2).

14. Williams, *Culture and Society 1780–1850,* p. 36.

15. Ibid., p. 47.

V: Poststructuralism and Academic Criticism

1. Frye, *Anatomy of Criticism,* pp. 117–18. Frank Lentricchia also uses this passage to contrast Frye to Derrida in *After the New Criticism,* pp. 14–16. See also pp. 24–26, where Lentricchia suggests that the *Anatomy* self-deconstructs.

2. Northrop Frye, *The Great Code* (New York: Harcourt Brace Jovanovich, 1981), p. xiv.

3. Brooks, *The Well-Wrought Urn*, pp. 214, 195. "Point of rest" is Robert Penn Warren's phrase, from "Pure and Impure Poetry" (1943), in *Critical Theory Since Plato*, ed. Hazard Adams (New York: Harcourt Brace Jovanovich, 1971), p. 991.

4. Stanley E. Fish, "Interpreting 'Interpreting the *Variorum*,'" *Critical Inquiry* 3 (Autumn 1976): 195–96. As I go on to show, many other contemporary critics think that accountability to the meaning of a text prevents freedom, creativity, and pleasure in interpretation. In addition to the critics cited in the text, see especially Roland Barthes, *The Pleasure of the Text*, trans. Richard Miller (New York: Hill and Wang, 1975), and several recent essays by Cary Nelson, including "Reading Criticism," *PMLA* 91 (October 1976): 801–15. The latter exemplifies the weaknesses of many of these arguments, including an inflated, self-congratulatory sense of opposition to academic criticism (this in an essay published in *PMLA!*); a reliance on distinctions that the author says he has discredited (after reducing objectivity to a strategic pose, Nelson can assert that the historical theses of Frye, Georges Poulet, and others are "obviously" mixtures of "fact and distortion"); and, finally, a tendency to deal in extremes (if there are "no decisively privileged vantage points," then rational evaluation is impossible; if interpretation is not "exclusively" detached, "altogether disinterested," "wholly impersonal (and thereby universal)," then it is personal, and "the value of identifying the critic in his criticism is much greater than the value of deciding which theories [here, of literary history] are correct and which are not"). See "Reading Criticism," 804, 810, 807.

5. Michael Ryan, "Self-Evidence," *Diacritics* 10 (Summer 1980): 5, 10.

6. Robert Crosman, "Do Readers Make Meaning?" in *The Reader in the Text*, ed. Susan R. Suleiman and Inge Crosman (Princeton: Princeton University Press, 1980), p. 162. Earlier Crosman calls belief in the determinacy of meaning "unsuited to modern democracy" but appropriate to the authoritarianism of the academic profession, with "its hierarchical structure of students, teachers, departments of literature, of less and more prestigious universities, journals, critical reputations." When we realize that readers make meanings, that a text "really means whatever any reader seriously believes it to mean," we will presumably replace the "war of all against all" with "tolerance," "mutual respect," and "the easy equality of friends." A compendium of clichés about the liberating value of recent theory, Crosman's article deserves to be quoted at even greater length than I have been able to do here.

7. Jonathan Arac, "History and Mystery: The Criticism of Frank Kermode," *Salmagundi* 55 (Winter 1982): 152.

8. I paraphrase here Frank Lentricchia's commentary on Michel Foucault, in *After the New Criticism*, pp. 175–76, 190–99.

9. Gayatri Chakravorty Spivak, "Translator's Preface" to *Of Grammatology*, p. lxxvii.

10. Bloom, *Poetry and Repression*, pp. 6–7.

11. The exchange between Hall and Hartman takes place in the Forum section of *PMLA* 94 (January 1979): 139–41, a fertile source of debates between deconstructive critics and their readers. See, for instance, Margreta de Grazia's excellent reply to Ronald Levao's "Sidney's Feigned *Apology*" in *PMLA* 94 (October 1979): 953–54. De Grazia zeroes in on the invulnerability of Levao's deconstructive logic: because he is convinced at the outset that

Sidney's text is "intentionally heterogeneous and contradictory," any "exceptions and counter examples" she adduces can be accommodated, even added "to the complexity and variety of the desired discovery." Nevertheless, de Grazia effectively points out the distortions that result when, like Levao, we treat casually an author's intention, a text's historical context, and relevant primary and secondary sources.

12. Derrida, "Limited Inc," p. 250. The examples are mine.

13. Murray Krieger, *Poetic Presence and Illusion* (Baltimore: The Johns Hopkins University Press, 1979), pp. 108–109. Like embarrassed parents, Cleanth Brooks and René Wellek have disclaimed responsibility for what they see as the "new apocalyptic irrationalism" (Wellek's term) of the critics who have succeeded them at Yale. See, for instance, Wellek's "The New Criticism: Pro and Contra," *Critical Inquiry* 4 (Summer 1978): 620–21. W. K. Wimsatt never lived to write about deconstruction, but he did criticize some of the structuralist and phenomenological developments that anticipated it in his last book, *Day of the Leopards: Essays in Defense of Poems* (New Haven: Yale University Press, 1976). See especially the essay "Battering the Object."

14. Peter Shaw, "Degenerate Criticism," *Harper's*, October 1979, 99. Digging one's own grave is Wayne C. Booth's metaphor for deconstruction in "'Preserving the Exemplar': or, How Not to Dig Our Own Graves," *Critical Inquiry* 3 (Spring 1977): 407–23.

15. William E. Cain notes in "Deconstruction in America" that "Miller's deconstructive stance not only privileges 'literature' but also—again one senses the conservatism—reifies the literary canon as it now stands." Though the terms of Miller's judgments have changed, he retains "the privilege granted to certain writers by literary history as it is usually written" (379). Cain goes on to remark "how easily all of this 'radical' material has been absorbed into the academic mainstream" (381): far from "being threatened and subverted by deconstruction," the institution of literary study has become "its long-lost center . . ." (382).

16. Conarroe does not mention the context of these references; maybe the papers cited these critics to disagree with them. But I doubt it. See the Editor's Column, *PMLA* 95 (January 1980): 3–4.

17. On the links between deconstruction and the New Criticism, see Graff, *Literature Against Itself,* p. 6. Graff realizes that the New Critics claimed knowledge for literature and criticism. But he notes that the premises of these critics are at odds with their intentions. Graff's analysis should be distinguished from the deconstructionists' appeal beyond a writer's stated intention. Graff opposes the aims of the New Critics to *their* ideas, not to the all-embracing effects of language. Frank Kermode also detects continuity between recent theory and the New Criticism it claims to leave behind. Both movements agree on the need for interpretation, on the necessity, in Kermode's words, of weaning lay readers "from the habit of literal reading." The university, Kermode rightly suggests, encourages such an attitude: as teachers, "we are in the business of conducting readers out of the sphere of the manifest." See "Institutional Control of Interpretation," 72–86.

18. Brooks, *The Well-Wrought Urn,* p. 199.

19. Lentricchia, *After the New Criticism,* p. 5.

20. See Bloom's review of *The Secular Scripture* in the *New York Times Book Review,* April 18, 1976, p. 21.

21. Derrida, *Of Grammatology,* pp. 158–59.

22. Miller, "Stevens' Rock and Criticism as Cure, II," 337.

23. See Christopher Ricks's review of Bloom's *Poetry and Repression* in the *New York Times Book Review*, March 14, 1976, p. 6.

24. Denis Donoghue, "Deconstructing Deconstruction," *The New York Review of Books*, June 12, 1980, p. 41. Other critics who have noticed compatibility between recent theory and the academic profession it attacks include Edward Said in "Reflections on Recent American 'Left' Literary Criticism," *Boundary 2*, 8 (Fall 1979): 11–30 (see especially pp. 12, 16 on Bloom and de Man); Donald Marshall, who in "The Inflation of Theory" notes that "de Man's and Derrida's chatter about death, violence, sex, and the void might give a transitory thrill to a numbed academic, long cloistered among adolescents" (*The Partisan Review* 48 [1981]: 296); and Hayden White, who calls Paul de Man "the academic critic's academic critic" ("Critic, Critic," *The Partisan Review* 48 [1981]: 311).

25. Of the numerous studies of professionalism, I have found most helpful Magali Sarfatti Larson, *The Rise of Professionalism* (Berkeley: University of California Press, 1977); Burton J. Bledstein, *The Culture of Professionalism* (New York: W. W. Norton, 1976); and Christopher Lasch, *Haven in a Heartless World* (New York: Basic Books, 1977).

26. Frederick Crews, *Out of My System* (New York: Oxford University Press, 1975), pp. 116–17.

27. In "Sparrows and Scholars: Literary Criticism and the Sanctification of Data," *The Georgia Review* 33 (Summer 1979): 255–76, Harold Fromm analyzes our "forlorn hope" that by expanding the quantity of criticism, we will somehow guarantee its importance.

28. Angus Fletcher, "The Perpetual Error," *Diacritics* 2 (Winter 1972): 20.

29. Graff, *Literature Against Itself*, p. 97. In "Institutional Control of Interpretation," Frank Kermode similarly observes that "the institution [of literary study] does not resist, rather encourages change; but it monitors change with very sophisticated machinery" (85). In a time of uncertainty, however, we monitor change less confidently: hence our susceptibility to fashion.

30. This compliment may seem like a sop. My complaint against Hartman, Bloom, and the others that I mention in this chapter, however, is not that they criticize academic criticism but that they nullify their own accusations, many of which seem to me justified.

31. The standards that Hartman ridicules are, however, clear enough for him to apply. In the exchange already cited, he complains that Hall "is not all that objective" when he quotes *Beyond Formalism* out of context. Maybe Hartman is being ironic, playfully faulting Hall for violating his own rules. But elsewhere he blames Hall's critique for not trying "to understand the perspective and critical styles it attacks"—an accusation that would seem to value the detachment that he questions. As in Derrida's reply to Searle, the same writer who "problematizes" objectivity also attaches great weight to achieving it—when someone else misunderstands his work.

32. I should add that Derrida has taken part in such projects as the Groupe de recherches sur l'enseignement philosophique (GREPH), which has protested against changes in the French educational system that would reduce the role of philosophy. But such political involvement, I would argue, occurs despite, not because of, the pessimistic tendencies in deconstruction that I have been analyzing. On Derrida's hopelessness, see also Frank Lentricchia, "Derrida, History, and Intellectuals," *Salmagundi* 50–51 (Fall 1980–Winter 1981): 284–301. I do not see why Lentricchia (in *After the New Criticism*) exempts Foucault from the accusations he directs in *Salmagundi* against Derrida:

both thinkers seem to me to leave us with an infinite regress of repressive discursive formations that makes resistance futile (or "problematic"). For both Foucault and Derrida, despite their other differences, humanity "installs each of its violences in a system of rules and then proceeds from domination to domination," as Foucault puts it in "Nietzsche, Genealogy, History," quoted in *After the New Criticism,* p. 203.

33. J. Hillis Miller, "Theory and Practice: Response to Vincent Leitch," *Critical Inquiry* 6 (Summer 1980): 612–13. Similarly, Hartman shrewdly observes that for de Man, "*language* rather than politics is fate; politics is part of a counterfeit Great Tradition that arrogates to itself the impositional strength of performative language" (*CW,* 108).

VI: Does Deconstruction Make Any Difference?

1. On the importance of the political action that I have in mind here, see my "The Literary Importance of E. P. Thompson's Marxism," *ELH* 50 (Winter 1983): 811–29.

2. For a widely read example of the "conservative" response to deconstruction, see Walter Jackson Bate, "The Crisis in English Studies," *Harvard Magazine,* September–October 1982, 46–53. Paul de Man's "The Return to Philology," *TLS,* December 10, 1982, 1355–56—in part, a reply to Bate—defends deconstruction as "close reading."

3. Christopher Norris, *Deconstruction Theory and Practice* (London and New York: Methuen, 1982), p. xii. Subsequent references are to page number. I may seem here to be putting too much emphasis on Norris's book, which is largely an introduction to deconstruction. But I am less interested in Norris's description of deconstruction than I am in the claims he makes on behalf of its subversiveness. These claims—which I want to question here—have dominated the consideration of deconstruction, at least by American critics.

4. Vincent B. Leitch, *Deconstructive Criticism* (New York: Columbia University Press, 1983), p. xii. Unlike Leitch, I have not been trying to piece together a comprehensive overview of deconstruction or of the individual critics that I discuss, preferring instead to concentrate on the assumptions that motivate (and defuse) the protest against academic criticism. While these assumptions do not sufficiently characterize deconstruction, I would argue that they are necessary to a definition of it. On the difficulty of representing deconstruction, see above, pp. 131–32, n. 18, and below, p. 139, n. 8.

5. Like Fish and Miller, numerous contemporary critics think that the endlessness of criticism militates against its truth claims. "Dismayed by the proliferation of interpretations," literary critics, in this view, who seek to "make [literary criticism] a true discipline" also "invoke the hope of saying the last word, arresting the process of commentary." (I quote from Jonathan Culler's *On Deconstruction* [Ithaca: Cornell University Press, 1982], p. 90.) But assigning criticism an end (i.e., an aim such as the discovery of a text's meaning) does not necessarily mean wishing to end criticism, as the example of Wayne C. Booth's *Critical Understanding* (Chicago: University of Chicago Press, 1979) shows. Far from being "dismayed by the proliferation of interpretations," Booth's pluralism legitimizes it. Instead of "arresting the process of commentary," Booth gives it a cognitive point. Lacking such a rationale, the production of criticism seems an end in itself, sustained, it would appear, by

inertia and by the institutional rewards it brings individual critics. Subsequent references to *On Deconstruction* are to the page number.

6. For further discussion of this obviously important topic, see George Lakoff and Mark Johnson, *Metaphors We Live By* (Chicago: University of Chicago Press, 1980). I might add that heightened sensitivity to metaphor, especially in extraliterary writing, seems to me an important contribution of poststructuralist theory. The classic deconstructionist treatment of this topic is Derrida's "White Mythology: Metaphor in the Text of Philosophy," in *Margins of Philosophy*, trans. Alan Bass (Chicago: University of Chicago Press, 1982), pp. 207–72. For a sympathetic commentary on Derrida's effort, see Richard Rorty, "Philosophy as a Kind of Writing: An Essay on Derrida," in *Consequences of Pragmatism* (Minneapolis: University of Minnesota Press, 1982), pp. 90–109.

7. Obviously this passage disturbs me (I have quoted it more than once): in my opinion, a critic who can make such a sweeping statement is not skeptical but omniscient. In *On Deconstruction,* Jonathan Culler concedes that "one cannot even imagine how [de Man] might argue for . . . the claim that nothing ever happens in any relation to anything that precedes, follows, or exists elsewhere." But Culler goes on to derive de Man's magisterial pronouncement here from "a certain faith in the text and the truth of its most fundamental and surprising implications . . . when exhaustively read" (280). In chapter 4 I try to show how the highly questionable conclusion that de Man attributes to *The Triumph of Life* results from his distorting it, not from his blindly trusting what it says.

8. Like Culler's *On Deconstruction,* Leitch's *Deconstructive Criticism,* although lauding deconstruction for "crumbling" all categories that evoke presence, nevertheless "aims to portray deconstruction clearly, concisely, and comprehensively" (ix). The persistence of notions like clarity, concision, and comprehensiveness—even in books sympathetic to deconstruction—leads me to question whether these norms have been "undone" (or whether they ought to be undone). Leitch acknowledges that "strictly speaking, to write a *book* on deconstruction should not be possible" because deconstruction "undermines the very notion *book,* offering in its place a radical form nicknamed *text*" (xii). But, he continues, "our present vantage and aim . . . compel us to repeat the book and to delay the move beyond it" (xii). I am not sure why Leitch expects to "move beyond" the book if, as he says elsewhere, for deconstruction "any 'beyond' is already 'in place' inside," and "repetition replaces revolution" (197).

9. J. Hillis Miller, "The Function of Rhetorical Study at the Present Time," in *The State of the Discipline 1970s–1980s,* ed. Jaspar P. Neel (New York: Association of Departments of English, 1979), p. 12. Subsequent references are to page number.

10. Jonathan Culler, *The Pursuit of Signs* (Ithaca: Cornell University Press, 1981), pp. 213, 217.

INDEX

Abrams, M. H.: on deconstruction, 41–42, 131nn. 13, 14; on *The Triumph of Life*, 61–63, 69, 77, 81

Academic criticism: crisis of, xi–xii, 101–102, 109, 122; and deconstruction, xi–xiii, 32, 83–109, 122–25; development of, 98–101

Altieri, Charles, 131nn. 13, 16, 133n.26

Arac, Jonathan, 87

Arnold, Matthew: and contemporary criticism, xiii, 1–3, 12–13, 29–30, 110–11; defense of poetry, 3–13; on the truth of poetry, 7–10; politics of, 10–12; compared to Northrop Frye, 17, 21

Baker, Carlos, 61, 70, 81

Barth, John, 23

Barthes, Roland, 93, 115, 119, 135n.4

Bate, Walter Jackson, 138n.2

Beardsley, Monroe, 47–48

Blake, William: 15–16, 18, 20, 25, 49. *See also* Romanticism

Bledstein, Burton, 137n.25

Bloom, Harold: on literary meaning, xi, 43–44, 59; on Matthew Arnold, 13; contrasted to Northrop Frye, 22, 95; compared to J. Hillis Miller, 54; reading of *The Triumph of Life*, 60, 62–63, 69–73, 80–82; critique of academic criticism, 87–88, 97, 104–106; theory of influence, 122

Booth, Wayne C., 34–35, 47, 56, 129n.27, 138n.5

Brooks, Cleanth, 16, 85, 92–94

Buckley, Vincent, 126n.11

Cain, William E., 131n.8, 133n.25, 136n.15

Cameron, Kenneth Neill, 61

Carlyle, Thomas, 17

Cavell, Stanley, xiv, 132n.23

Cobbett, William, 5

Conarroe, Joel, 93

Convention, 34, 88, 90–91, 118–19, 132n.23

Crews, Frederick, 101

Crosman, Robert, 87

Culler, Jonathan, 103, 120–21, 123, 131n.16, 138n.5, 139n.7

Defense of poetry: preconditions of, xiv, 9–10, 12, 29, 110–11. *See also* Matthew Arnold, Northrop Frye

De Grazia, Margreta, 135n.11

De Man, Paul: reading of *The Triumph of Life*, 35, 61, 63–67, 69–70, 73–76, 80–82; style of, 103; politics of, 108, 119, 138n.33; on metaphor, 116; mentioned, 93, 95, 138n.2

Denham, R. D., 130n.36

Derrida, Jacques: on literary meaning, 32–43, 58–59, 72, 106, 114, 116, 137n.31; compared to Stanley Fish, 44–45, 132n.18; critique of academic criticism, 90–92, 103–104, 106–107; and the New Criticism, 93–94; as formalist, 95–97; politics of, 108, 118–19; on metaphor, 116, 139n.6; mentioned, 52–54, 93, 95, 111–12

Dickstein, Morris, 2–3, 12–13

Différance, 34, 114

Donoghue, Denis, 97, 134n.8

Eagleton, Terry, 116

Eliot, T. S., 15, 127n.13

Ellis, John, 50–51, 131n.16

Equality, 10–12, 19–20, 30–31, 111

Erdman, David, 78

Fish, Stanley: on literary meaning, xi, 44–51, 58–59; compared to Jacques Derrida, 44–45, 132n.18; critique of academic criticism, 86–87, 123

Fletcher, Angus, 103

Formalism, 86, 93, 95–97

Foucault, Michel, 23, 93, 137n.32

Freud, Sigmund, xiii, 18

Fromm, Harold, 137n.27

Frye, Northrop: related to deconstruction, xiii, 13, 23, 29–31, 94–95, 110–11; de-